REAL LIFE
~ on ~
CANNERY ROW

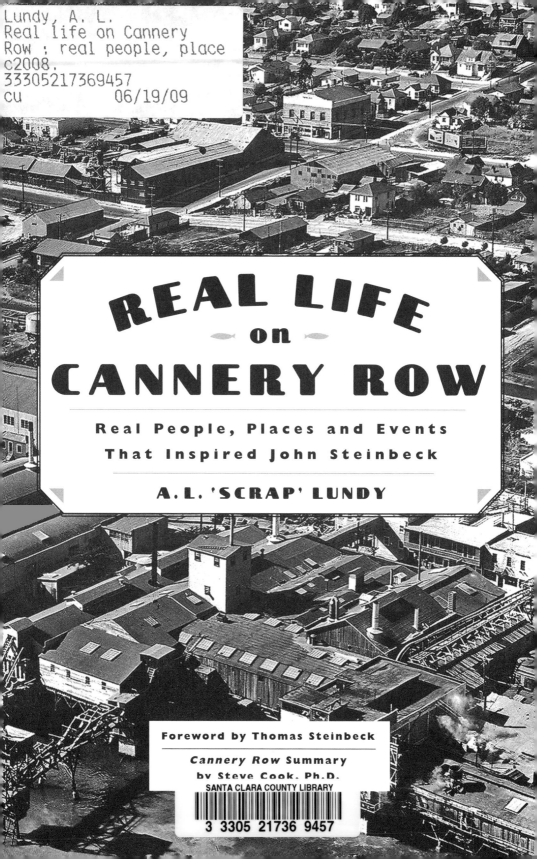

REAL LIFE
~ on ~
CANNERY ROW

Real People, Places and Events
That Inspired John Steinbeck

A. L. 'SCRAP' LUNDY

Foreword by Thomas Steinbeck

Cannery Row Summary
by Steve Cook, Ph.D.

PUBLISHED BY ANGEL CITY PRESS
2118 Wilshire Blvd. #880, Santa Monica, California 90403 U.S.A.
+1.310.395.9982   www.angelcitypress.com

10 9 8 7 6 5 4 3 2 1
ISBN-13 978-1-883318-90-1 / ISBN-10 1-883318-90-4

Excerpts used in this book are used with permission and credited to the following:

The True Adventures of John Steinbeck, Writer by Jackson J. Benson, copyright © 1984 by Jackson J. Benson. Used by permission of Viking Penguin, a division of Penguin Group (USA) Inc.

The Log from the Sea of Cortez by John Steinbeck, copyright © 1941, 1951 by John Steinbeck and E.F. Ricketts. Copyright renewed 1969, by John Steinbeck and Edward F. Ricketts, Jr. Used by permission of Viking Penguin, a division of Penguin Group (USA) Inc.

Cannery Row by John Steinbeck, copyright © 1945 by John Steinbeck. Copyright renewed 1973, by Elaine Steinbeck, John Steinbeck, John Steinbeck IV and Thom Steinbeck. Used by permission of Viking Penguin, a division of Penguin Group (USA) Inc.

Steinbeck Remembered by Audry Lynch, copyright © 2002. Used by permission of Daniels and Daniels Publishers, Inc.

John Steinbeck and Edward F. Ricketts: the Shaping of a Novelist by Richard Astro, copyright © 1976. Used by permission of University of Minnesota Press.

Except as noted in captions, photographs in this book are from the author's collection.

Cover photos: Ed Ricketts (top left), Flora Woods (top right) and aerial view of Cannery Row courtesy of California Views: The Pat Hathaway Photo Collection; Peter Stackpole photograph of Harold "Gabe" Bicknell courtesy of the Martha Heasley Cox Center for Steinbeck Studies, San Jose State University.

DESIGN BY KATHY KIKKERT

LIBRARY OF CONGRESS CATALOGING-IN-PUBLICATION DATA
Lundy, A. L.
  Real life on Cannery Row : real people, places and events that inspired John Steinbeck / by A.L. "Scrap" Lundy ; foreword by Thomas Steinbeck ; introduction by Michael K. Hemp.
     p. cm.
  Includes bibliographical references and index.
  Summary: "A timeless tour through John Steinbeck's world, REAL LIFE ON CANNERY ROW highlights the unique individuals and memorable moments that influenced Steinbeck's iconic novel. Characters from the novel are brought to life, showcasing true stories behind fictional events. The book offers essential insight into CANNERY ROW and is a helpful companion piece for Steinbeck students and fans"--Provided by publisher.
  ISBN 978-1-883318-90-1 (trade paper : alk. paper)
  1. Steinbeck, John, 1902-1968. Cannery Row. 2. Steinbeck, John, 1902-1968--Characters. I. Title.

PS3537.T3234C47 2008
813'.52--dc22

                          2008040990

Printed in the United States of America

ANGEL CITY PRESS

To the residents of Cannery Row and the Monterey area, who provided the inspiration for John Steinbeck to write CANNERY ROW.

CONTENTS

PART THREE
EVENTS & HAPPENINGS

FOREWORD

MANY DEDICATED READERS, STUDENTS AND OTHER
aficionados of the more obscure origins of literary invention have often written inquiring letters, or even published dissertations that focused specifically upon the origins of Steinbeck's precisely drawn characters. Were his characters reflections of a familiar reality, or pure invention cobbled from bits and
pieces to fit a specific literary rationale?

As a writer I would be remiss to suggest that it was anything other than all
of the above. But for John Steinbeck, who was a socially attuned journalist at
heart, external realities held far more interest than pure invention. Therefore,
like young Da Vinci sketching informal portraits on the streets of Florence,
Steinbeck preferred to explore the realities expressed in the everyday lives,
motives and aspirations of the people he knew and observed. To that end, he
always showed a particular preference for the company and companionship
of working men and women. He enjoyed many happy mornings just sharing
java and sinkers with local friends down at the five-and-dime-cum-drugstore
lunch counter. There he'd trade off stories, ancient jokes, medical com-
plaints, and humorous political observations with local crab fishermen, hard-
ware salesmen, truck drivers, potato farmers, "gentlemen of the road,"
boat captains, postmen and almost anybody else with a mind to enter the
conversation.

Amidst all confabulation, Steinbeck always remained the empathetic listener, often contributing only those comments that he believed would amuse
and entertain his companions, and asking only those questions that presented his interlocutors with blank canvases on which to depict their innermost

viewpoints and opinions. He rarely shared his own private observations with anyone but close friends, and never debated the fine points of any subject with acquaintances. Among strangers, Steinbeck invariably remained a model of rural chivalry, honest hospitality and authentic good humor. This benign and enlightened approach encouraged most people to open up their lives with greater expectation of receiving an unbiased audience. In this respect they were rarely if ever disappointed.

In the following volume, Scrap Lundy has given us a remarkably detailed history of some of the people that Steinbeck portrayed in his earliest works about Monterey, California, during the later part of the Great Depression. Mr. Lundy's detailed research, which includes in-depth interviews with those Cannery Row denizens who knew Steinbeck's character models well, is in itself a remarkable example of painstaking dedication to his subject.

Some of these characters, like Mack from *Cannery Row*, went on to become the breath and bones of a number of Steinbeck's characters in other stories and books; *The Raid* and *In Dubious Battle* stand out as prime examples, but there are instances of these uniquely faceted people reappearing, in one guise or another, in some of Steinbeck's later works.

For all those who share a fascination with John Steinbeck's *Cannery Row*, its intriguing history, and the unique characters brought forth in Steinbeck's early writing, this book will add colorful dimensions and insights that the reader will find most entertaining and informative. At the same time, the work also casts an interesting light on Steinbeck's ability to gauge and interpret the character and persona of others, and then portray those qualities accurately and honestly within the constraints of his novels. I recommend Mr. Lundy's book to all latent Steinbeck scholars and to those readers who have become fervent admirers of John Steinbeck's work over the years. I am convinced the reader will find a reply to the long-voiced question about the origins of Steinbeck's characters within these pages.

—THOMAS STEINBECK
Montecito, California
2008

INTRODUCTION

JACKSON J. BENSON, THE AUTHORIZED STEINBECK
biographer, was asked from the audience in Salinas at the 1984 Steinbeck
Festival—at the time of the publication of *The True Adventures of John Steinbeck,
Writer*—what he thought were John Steinbeck's most important works. Jack
responded, *Of Mice and Men, Grapes of Wrath* and . . . *Cannery Row*. A gasp from
the audience signaled astonishment that *Cannery Row* should be in such company. Years later, in the planning for the 2002 Steinbeck Centennial events,
Benson confirmed that recollection and added quite ardently that, in fact, of
all of Steinbeck's works, his hands-down personal favorite is *Cannery Row*.

That landmark recognition of *Cannery Row* has not, unfortunately, been
matched with the kinds of literary research that a subject with such substan-
tial historical requisites requires. That is, until now. Enter A.L. "Scrap" Lundy,
passionate researcher and published historian of the abalone industry in
California. A longtime member of the Historical Diving Society (USA),
Lundy wrote *The California Abalone Industry—A Pictorial History*, which stands as
the seminal work on the industry and its Japanese practitioners, many of
whom operated from the shores of Monterey Bay.

Ed Ricketts would call it a synchronicity—abalone and the Japanese and
Cannery Row—tied together by a novelist and a scientist. During his vora-
cious immersion in his newfound field of the largely unexamined history of
Cannery Row, Scrap and I met at a Steinbeck Festival, then still held in
Sherwood Hall at the Salinas Fairgrounds. *Cannery Row*—the book and the
place—not only became a passion for Scrap, but he developed a particularly
insatiable need to know who these people were in the book, and whether the

locations were real or not. We fell into each other's worlds on the spot. I've spent time with him at the Monterey County Clerk's office in Salinas, at microfiche and huge leather-bound record books whose pages gave up voluminous details of compelling interest only to us "true believers."

Scrap soon found that John Steinbeck's *Cannery Row* not only passed for history in Monterey, it also created decades of local folklore in America's old sardine capital, with both claims and presumptions as to who many of its characters were—or were not. Nor were actual Cannery Row locations exempt from stretches of the imagination, sometimes-wild guesses, and flights of fancy or pure ignorance as Steinbeck readers interpreted the artifice of his craft. Even the best-intentioned readers can err in the urge to identify the person or the place Steinbeck meant. Others, who may know something of Cannery Row, frequently add their own fanciful or uninformed conclusions. The result has been a heritage of hearsay, embellishment and occasional controversy on all counts, without any authoritative basis to establish historical fact about John Steinbeck's masterful sea of fiction.

The simple truth is that John Steinbeck didn't write much pure fiction. Real people and real places come alive in his Monterey works, starting with *Tortilla Flat.* But *Cannery Row* is perhaps his most ambitious and diverse use of real people and places in the construction of a story.

Much of the confusion over the decades, at least in regard to the real locations that have obvious *Cannery Row* correlations, has been made more chaotic given the lack of historical markers on Cannery Row itself. It is incredible—perhaps unforgivable—that only the Cannery Row Foundation's Edward F. Ricketts Memorial and one small family-sponsored plaque at the site of California Frozen Fish Company are the only historic markers in one of the most important districts in American history and world literature. Further, only two structures in the entire Cannery Row district are listed on the National Register of Historic Places: Ed Ricketts' Lab (Pacific Biological Laboratories) and the warehouse of the Carmel Canning Company, a block above Cannery Row on Wave Street.

The questions remain, however, "So what?" So what if Steinbeck used real people or not, real places or not? To many it doesn't matter at all. But to those who are touched by the genius of Steinbeck's words on a page, it is critically important. Beyond that, Ed Ricketts—John's closest friend, mentor, alter ego, and model for six major characters in his fiction—would care most about "what is." That, simply is reason enough for Scrap Lundy to have spent eleven years on the research that is about to be spread before you by a true believer with no other real motivation than to set the record straight.

You are about to find out more from an historical point of view than academic America knows about John Steinbeck and *Cannery Row*. You are about to engage in the joy of understanding and appreciation of a talent not given frequently to readers. I invite you to enjoy and indeed, savor Scrap Lundy's passion in this indispensable companion to the reading of John Steinbeck's *Cannery Row*.

MICHAEL K. HEMP
Founder, Cannery Row Foundation

PREFACE

JOHN STEINBECK OPENED *CANNERY ROW* **WITH THE WORDS** "The people, places and events in this book are, of course, fictions and fabrications." *Of course?* Thirteen years after the book was published, Steinbeck wrote in a letter, "The book is only fiction in form and style." That being said, I took the challenge to find out how much was actually fact and how much was fiction.

Real Life on Cannery Row was originally conceived as a companion piece to the 1945 novel. It approaches the story of *Cannery Row* from a perspective that has never been attempted, a view that provides readers with information on who and what the real people, places and events were in an area of Monterey, California, called Cannery Row, that wonderful *real* place that inspired John Steinbeck to create his iconic work of fiction.

By learning about the true personalities and backgrounds of the real people the author knew and upon whom he based his principal characters, Steinbeck's readers may develop an understanding and a sense of connection with his characters, a way to make reading *Cannery Row* even more enjoyable. The same holds true for the places depicted in the book. Knowing that most of the locations mentioned are real and still can be visited only adds to the vitality of the novel. Knowing the true relationship between John Steinbeck and a group of the real people existing in real places allows the reader to enter Cannery Row just as Steinbeck did, first literally, then imaginatively.

The results of the eleven years of research I conducted clearly show that almost every character, place and event were based in reality. From there, Steinbeck created the fictional story that only he could create. Steinbeck's changes to real people and situations were sometimes relatively minor in nature, but he wrapped a masterful story around them, creating the book that has gone on to become a classic of American literature. It was a mark of his genius that he was able to meld reality and fiction into a novel that was at once perfectly complex and perfectly simple.

His ability to blend fact and fiction was especially significant when it came to his characters. Real people doing real things became the basis of the fictional world that was Steinbeck's *Cannery Row*—Ed Ricketts, Flora Woods and Gabe Bicknell were prototypes for the novel's Doc, Dora, and Mack. When Gay (who also was based on Steinbeck's friend, the Row-local Gabe Bicknell) left the boys to get car parts so they could continue on a frog hunt in Chapter Fifteen, Steinbeck was anchored in a real-life occurrence. Along the way, Gay got drunk in Jimmy Brucia's bar, broke a window in Holman's Bootery and passed out on a lounge in the display window. Gabe's daughter, Dottie, confirmed the Holman's story really happened, but she said the window was broken at Holman's store in Pacific Grove, not in Monterey. Steinbeck used the Holman's Alvarado Street store because it was closer to Jimmy Brucia's bar. Such modest alterations of the facts only add to the entertainment value of the incident while still honoring its reality.

Though most of Steinbeck's characters are based directly on real people, some seem to have been pure invention, strokes of Steinbeck's genius. Consider Hazel, a friend of Doc and one of the "boys." Steinbeck introduces Hazel in Chapter Six during a specimen-collecting trip with Doc. Steinbeck develops a detailed personality for Hazel—he tells how Hazel went to both grammar and reform schools, but "didn't learn anything in either place" and "came out of reform school as innocent of viciousness as he was of fractions." Steinbeck also described how he "asked questions, not to hear the answers but simply to continue the flow [of conversation]." This particular quality made Hazel the perfect early companion for Doc—his inquisitive personality allowed Doc's philosophic and thoughtful nature to shine. There seems to be no real-life reference for Hazel's character, but one can easily see why Steinbeck chose to invent him. Hazel is the perfect foil for both Doc and Mack, drawing out their personalities and helping Steinbeck show, not tell, his characters' true colors. Hazel proves that while Steinbeck drew heavily on real life for his novel, he was still a master craftsman and ingenious fiction writer.

The gestation period of this book began in 1995, but I was totally unaware that it was happening. In the early- to mid-1990s, I traveled to Monterey frequently to conduct research for my first book, *The California Abalone Industry—A Pictorial History*. In the course of the research, I had the good fortune to meet members of the Cannery Row Foundation, namely Bonnie Gartshore, Pat Hathaway, Neal and Bettina Hotelling, Kalisa Moore and Dr. Susan Shillinglaw.

The Foundation members invited me to speak on a historical topic at an upcoming seminar. Until then, I had not read *Cannery Row* nor, for that matter, any of Steinbeck's books. Not wanting to feel like a complete outsider, I quickly read it. I was completely taken by Steinbeck's writing style for two reasons. First, he was able to describe a scene so clearly that I felt I was almost part of it. Second, like so many Steinbeck readers, I was greatly impressed by the way he portrayed characters, both their attributes and frailties, with unconditional acceptance. From that point forward it made sense to me when someone like Abby Pfeiffer, the grant writer for the National Steinbeck Center in Salinas, told me, "I feel safe reading John Steinbeck and I'm sad when the book ends, as I feel like I'm losing my new friends." I understood completely.

During subsequent trips to Monterey, I learned of the existence of several places that had been used in the book. I found Lee Chong's, Steinbeck's fictionalized market that was based on the real Wing Chong Co., Doc's Lab (based on Ed Ricketts' lab) and La Ida (until 2007, Kalisa's). After I discovered where those buildings were located, I recall feeling connected with the story—a good feeling, one I wanted to have again. Because I have a natural interest in researching historical events, I kept wondering what else could be real.

To research the people, places and events in *Cannery Row*, I had to know their names. To that end, I read *Cannery Row* four more times, and with each reading I underlined another person, place or event I felt merited investigation. After the fourth reading, I counted 133 topics, and it was at that point I decided it was time to stop reading and to start researching.

When I started, I had just finished my first book, which meant I would be able to use the same methods I had previously found to be so useful. For both books, my three main sources of information were various public records, interviews with people who were involved in the events related in the books, and newspaper articles. I found the following sources to be very helpful: For marriage licenses, death and birth certificates and property transfers, I relied on the wonderful staff at the Monterey County Clerk's Office in Salinas. To research older Monterey, I used city directories, phone books, *Polk* directories and newspaper articles, ably aided by Dennis Copeland, archivist of the excellent California Room Archives in the Monterey Public Library.

To understand the connections between the book's characters and the real people of Cannery Row, the most interesting and valuable sources proved to be the many folks I interviewed who had lived at the time of the book's setting and were still available to discuss those amazing days. Among that group, the most informative were the people who, in addition to having lived in Cannery Row, knew the prototypes for the book's three main characters: Ed Ricketts (who was the inspiration for Steinbeck's Doc), Flora Woods (Dora Flood), and the aforementioned Gabe Bicknell (Mack and Gay).

It is true that the passage of time may erode a person's memory. To offset such a possibility, I always tried to doublecheck a relevant piece of information by asking others who were knowledgeable about it. In other words, to warrant using a particular bit of verbal recollection, I did my utmost to substantiate the story with at least one other person's recollection.

Of all the wonderful people I interviewed, Dottie Bicknell Sanchez was the most informative. Not only had she known two of the three main characters, Ed Ricketts and Flora Woods, but she is also the daughter of Gabe Bicknell. She astounded me several times by relating several of her father's antics exactly as Steinbeck portrayed Mack and Gay doing them in the book. She was also a great source of information on how life on the Row really was. For example, Dottie and Jimmy Rodriquez, a policeman who patrolled

Cannery Row during this time, both confirmed that people really did sleep in the discarded pipes and boilers. Their names may not have been Malloy, as in the book, but they were real people.

After completing sixteen years of research for the two books, I can say with little reservation that newspaper articles were the least reliable sources of information. Although I read as many articles as I could find, I discovered some articles consisted of pure fiction written by journalists who neither knew the facts nor cared to verify their findings. Too often I found that over time bad reporting became represented as fact.

After I discovered which sources I could trust, I learned that the vast majority of the book was based on fact, and I realized that there was another important element involved. The reason John Steinbeck was able to bring his characters to life and to make the world of *Cannery Row* so vivid and richly detailed is that he lived with these people. His honest portrayal of the strengths and weaknesses of his characters made them seem almost real because they *were* real. Surrounded by the rich abundance of life—both on the street and in the sea—that was Cannery Row, Steinbeck faithfully reflected the world around him, deciding simply, as he wrote, "to open the page and let the stories crawl in by themselves."

To the avid reader, I hope this book will enhance your reading experience. To the Steinbeck fan, may it bring Steinbeck himself into the story, may you see him sitting alongside his many interesting friends in the world he lived in called Cannery Row. With the information, maps and photos in this book, plus a little imagination, a *Cannery Row* enthusiast may be able to see many parts of the book come to life. I suggest that the best time for this literary experience is in what Steinbeck called the "hour of the pearl—the interval between day and night, when time stops and examines itself."

—A.L. "SCRAP" LUNDY
Santa Barbara
2008

Cannery Row

In the mid- to late 1930s, the name Cannery Row meant a certain area of New Monterey, outside of the historic downtown. In the 1930s and 1940s, Cannery Row was bordered on the west by David Avenue, on the south by Wave Street, on the north by Ocean View Avenue and on the east by Reeside Avenue. Locals called it Cannery Row because it contained practically all the sardine canneries in the area as well as their associated buildings.

In January of 1958, the waterfront street Ocean View Avenue—from Reeside Avenue to David Avenue—was officially renamed "Cannery Row" to honor Steinbeck's book. The business interests in Monterey hoped that revenue generated from tourists would replace the income lost when the sardines, and the silver tide they generated, disappeared in the late 1950s and early 1960s.

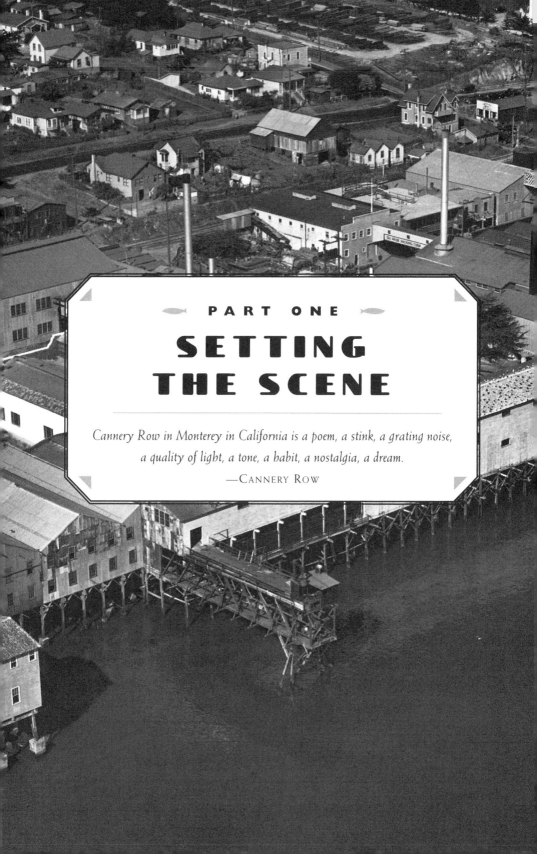

PART ONE

SETTING
THE SCENE

*Cannery Row in Monterey in California is a poem, a stink, a grating noise,
a quality of light, a tone, a habit, a nostalgia, a dream.*

—CANNERY ROW

DEL MAR CANNING CO.

1. Doc's / Ed's Lab
2. Dora's / Flora's
3. Chicken Walk
4. The Palace
5. Vacant Lot
6. Wing Chong's
7. La Ida / Kalisa's

1939. An aerial view of the Cannery Row area from Hovden's (Morden's) at the lower right corner to Reeside Avenue on the left side. Ocean View Avenue (now Cannery Row) is the street that is closest and parallel to the ocean. Ed's (in *Cannery Row*, Doc's) lab, Flora's (Dora's), the Palace, the vacant lot, the Wing Chong Co. (Lee Chong's grocery) and Kalisa's (La Ida) are visible near the smokestack at the right.

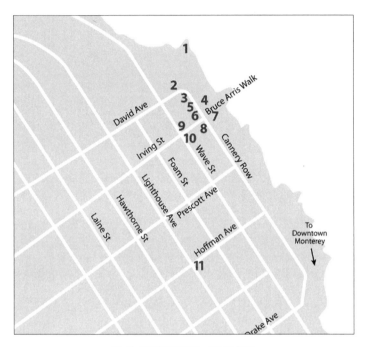

CANNERY ROW

1. China Point / Hopkins Marine Station
2. Hovden's Cannery (Morden's), now The Monterey Bay Aquarium
3. Kalisa's (La Ida Café), 851 Cannery Row, now a restaurant
4. Sea Pride Packing Company (Hediondo Cannery), 820 Cannery Row
5. The Wing Chong Co. (Lee Chong's Grocery), 835 Cannery Row
6. Vacant lot
7. Pacific Biological Laboratories (Western Biological Laboratory)
8. Flora's Lone Star Café (Dora's Bear Flag), 799 Cannery Row
9. Chicken Walk, now Bruce Ariss Way
10. Palace Flophouse, 798 Wave Street
11. Half-Way House (Halfway House), 598 Lighthouse Avenue

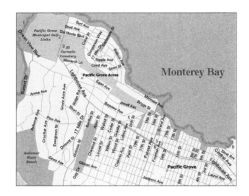

PACIFIC GROVE AREA

1. Great Tide Pools
2. Point Piños Lighthouse
3. El Carmelo Cemetery
   (The Pretty Little Cemetery)
4. Gabe Bicknell's House, 159 Pacific Street

5. Holman's Department Store,
   542 Lighthouse Avenue
6. Scotch Bakery, 545 Lighthouse Avenue
7. Red Williams' Flying A gas station
8. China Point / Hopkins Marine Station

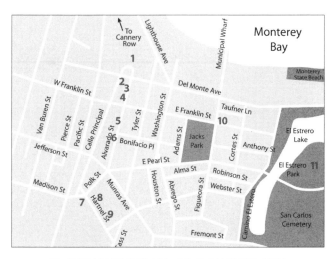

DOWNTOWN MONTEREY

1. Jimmy Brucia's Bar, 242 Alvarado
2. Palace Hotel and Palace Grill,
   315 and 319 Alvarado
3. El Adobe Bar, 324-326 Alvarado
4. Hermann's, 380 Alvarado
5. Holman's Bootery, 418 Alvarado
6. The Poppy (The Golden Poppy), 434 Alvarado

7. Stokes Adobe, 500 Hartnell
8. Hartnell Gulch
9. Post Office, 565 Hartnell
10. Golden Stairs, corner of Franklin
    and Figueroa Streets.
11. Hotel Del Monte

ca. 1936. Even somewhat formally attired in a coat, Ed Ricketts is wearing his ever-present magnifying glass, visible on his right lapel.

PAT HATHAWAY PHOTO COLLECTION

Doc would listen to any kind of nonsense and change it for you to a kind of wisdom . . . He lived in a world of wonders, of excitement.

—CHAPTER FIVE

CHAPTER 1

ED RICKETTS

THE CHARACTER JOHN STEINBECK CALLED "DOC" WAS BASED on a local scientist named Ed Ricketts, a fact that Steinbeck himself confirmed in *The Log from the Sea of Cortez*. He specifically made the point that he "used the laboratory, and Ed himself, in a book called *Cannery Row.*"

Edward F. Ricketts was born in Chicago, Illinois, on May 14, 1897. He graduated from high school in 1914, and then attended Illinois Normal University for a year. From 1917 to 1919, he worked at various jobs, including a year in the army during World War I. From mid-1919 to 1922, Ed took

1938. With help from Richie Lovejoy, who illustrated much of *Between Pacific Tides*, Ricketts is examining a skate.

classes at the University of Chicago in biology, philosophy, German and Spanish, but he did not graduate. Even though he never attained his degree, locals still called Ricketts "Doc," mostly because of the minor first aid he provided. Monterey resident Elena Young, who had known him when she was a young girl living on Cannery Row, recalls that "He was always very nice and good to us kids. We called him Doc, because he would fix our skinned knees." The moniker stuck.

His exposure to Dr. W.C. Allee, a professor of marine biology at the University of Chicago, proved to be a turning point in Ed's life and, by association, became important to Steinbeck. Allee visited the Hopkins Marine Station in Pacific Grove, California, where Ricketts worked prior to 1922, and taught Ed about the rich marine shore life in nearby Monterey. In these classes, Ed started to form his ideas of how creatures in tide pools act, whether individually or in a group. Over the years, Ed expanded his ideas on the subject, ideas that Steinbeck would later incorporate into his writing.

Ricketts married Anna (Nan) Maker on August 19, 1922 in Chicago. After Ed, Jr., was born in 1923, the new family moved to Pacific Grove, California. Ed and Nan had conflicting personalities, and the marriage was unhappy from the start. Nan preferred to stay at home and take care of the family, while Ed's adventurous spirit led him to socialize and travel.

Western Biological was right across the street and facing the vacant lot. Lee Chong's grocery was on its catty-corner right and Dora's Bear Flag Restaurant was on its catty-corner left. —CHAPTER FIVE

And Western Biological sells bugs and snails and spiders and rattlesnakes and rats and honey bees and gila monsters. —CHAPTER FIVE

In September of 1923, Ricketts and his college roommate, A.E. Galigher, opened the Pacific Biological Laboratories at 165 Fountain Avenue in Pacific Grove, which provided biological specimens to schools and other interested parties. Shortly after the lab's opening, Galigher left the business and Ed became the sole owner.

pre-1936. Ricketts' lab at 740 Ocean View Avenue
(800 Cannery Row) was destroyed by fire on November 25, 1936.
PAT HATHAWAY PHOTO COLLECTION

The lab provided Ricketts the place to conduct his business and research in marine biology. His seminal book, *Between Pacific Tides*, remains the primary reference on that topic. To make a living while writing, Ricketts collected,

1947. The "bedroom" of Ricketts' lab.

PAT HATHAWAY PHOTO COLLECTION

prepared and shipped a vast array of land-based and marine creatures to schools for use in biology and zoology classes. In addition to his tide pool animal specialty, Ed supplied cats, butterflies and frogs. He did a great deal of the collecting himself; however, at times he employed many helpers, including some of the more knowledgeable and competent homeless men, local kids and fishermen.

On July 28, 1928, Ed bought a fifty-foot-wide lot that held a well-built stucco house at 740 Ocean View Avenue (the address later changed to 800 Cannery Row). Because the building he had been using as a lab, at 165 Fountain Avenue, was torn down in 1927, Ed moved his lab to his Ocean View Avenue address. He continued to live with his family in Pacific Grove; however, due to marital problems, the family split up and, in 1932, Ed moved into the lab. He continued to live and work there until his death in 1948. To make the single-story structure more usable as a business, Ricketts had Pacific Grove contractor Roscoe Wright raise it and build a basement. The lab stands where Steinbeck placed it in the book, and still remains there— Steinbeck merely changed the name from the Pacific Biological Laboratories to the Western Biological Laboratory.

The building had two levels. The upper level contained Ricketts' living area, office, bed, kitchen and a storage area for the cages that contained rats and rattlesnakes. The rattlesnakes were kept in cages between the safe and the filing cabinet, and the rats were kept in another room.[1] Ed did most of the real lab work in the newly created basement. All the necessary equipment needed to prepare, store and ship the specimens was located there.

In the rattlesnake cage the snakes lay with their chins resting on their own coils . . . —CHAPTER TWENTY-ONE

Between rumors of fantastic specimens and first-hand accounts of Ed's kindness, the lab held an almost mythical status for residents of Monterey. Ed's remarkable personality gave the lab an ambiance that made it the friendliest place in Cannery Row. Any visitor, whether or not acquainted with Ed, would always be treated kindly and with respect, according to friends and locals who knew him.

Then there are little unborn humans, some whole and others sliced thin and mounted on slides. —CHAPTER FIVE

Residents often speculated about the "pickled babies" in Ricketts' lab. On occasion, he had embryos in bottles in his lab. When interviewed by Michael Hemp, the founder of the Cannery Row Foundation, Grace Bergara, the daughter of a local cannery worker, said, "I saw embryos in bottles and I called them pickled babies."[2] In "About Ed Ricketts," the preface to *The Log from the Sea of Cortez*, Steinbeck explained the source of an embryo that was the topic of conversation among area residents, especially the lucky ones who got to see it.

> For many years he [Ed's father] worked in the basement stockroom packing specimens to be shipped and even mounting some of the larger and less delicate forms. His chief pride, however, was a human fetus that he had mounted in a museum jar. It was to have been the lone child of a Negress and a Chinese. When the mother succumbed to a lover's quarrel and a large dose of arsenic administered by person or persons unknown, the authorities revealed her secret and her secret was acquired by Pacific Biological. It was much too advanced for study to be of much value so Ed's father inherited it. He crossed its little legs in a Buddha pose, arranged its hands in an attitude of semi-prayer. Children and many adults made pilgrimages to the basement to see it.

During the 1930s, Ricketts became a well-known and highly respected member of the Cannery Row community. He lived alone in the lab—he and his wife Nan had conflicts, so she and their son and daughters stayed at the house, and Ed never moved back home, yet the couple never divorced. Although Ed lived alone, he was never at a loss for company. According to Steinbeck, and others who visited Ed, social gatherings in the lab occurred fairly often. However, when there was work to be done, Ed did it. Ed, Jr., said that when his father had specimen orders to fill and ship, he would leave a gathering and go to the basement to work.

In *Cannery Row,* Steinbeck portrays Doc as a person who, despite his very strong work ethic, also enjoyed a flourishing social life. Indeed, Ed Ricketts sought out female companionship and also enjoyed drinking. As *Cannery Row* suggests, beer was one of Ed's favorite drinks. He liked Burgermeister beer, and Ed, Jr., said that after a trip with Steinbeck to Mexico in 1940, his father acquired a taste for Dos Equis, the Mexican beer.

Because of Ricketts' broad range of intellectual interests, the lab had always been a meeting place for local artists and writers, including artist Bruce Ariss, author Henry Miller, and mythologist Joseph Campbell. Ricketts and Steinbeck met in 1930 and, because they shared many interests, the two men developed a very close and lifelong friendship. Their topics of mutual interest included classical literature and music, philosophy and marine biology. Ed, Steinbeck and others, including Campbell, had regular gatherings in the lab and discussed the various merits of many profound topics. During this period Steinbeck encountered many of the people and observed events he would later use in *Cannery Row.*

Jackson J. Benson commented on the lab's visitors and their activities in *The True Adventures of John Steinbeck, Writer.* "Many of the same people dropped by the lab, plus Barbara and Ellwood Graham [a local artist] and occasionally one of the Steinbeck's more recent friends, Burgess Meredith [the actor] or Lewis Milestone [film director]. They sprawled out in Ed's office or in the living room/bedroom/library/music room next to it, drinking wine or beer, swapping stories and listening to records."

After Steinbeck completed *Cannery Row* in 1945 and prior to publication, he asked Ricketts to read it and make comments. Ed wrote his son, who was

Remembering Ed

In the course of researching this book, the author had the rare privilege of speaking to a number of people who knew Ed Ricketts in the 1930s and early 1940s. From their recollection of how Ed treated others, no matter their age or position in life, each person remembered Ed's rare ability to cause people to feel better about themselves after they spoke with him. Folks who knew Ed made the following comments:

FLORUS WILLIAMS, who often observed Ed in his brother Red's gas station said, "Ed was serious, very nice and great to kids."

JOE BRAGDON remembered Ed this way: "I was a cannery worker in the late 1930s. While I was waiting for the cannery whistle to blow, I'd go down and hang around Ricketts' lab. Ed was an easygoing person, quiet, unassuming and congenial. He was very good at explaining things as well as letting folks wander through."

JIMMY RODRIQUEZ, the policeman on the Cannery Row evening beat, saw Ed often and commented, "Ed was a quiet and very nice man. I never saw him intoxicated."

IRENE LONGUEIRA's comment may be the best of all: "He had room in his heart for everyone."

1940. Ricketts sits on a rock near the Hopkins Marine Station on Ocean View Boulevard in Pacific Grove.

PAT HATHAWAY PHOTO COLLECTION

1947. Ricketts sits in the dining area of the lab's upstairs, a space that was also his bedroom and library. The bottle on the table is Burgermeister, his favorite beer.

in the army at the time, "It's mostly about me. Because I occurred in it so obviously and so frequently, [Steinbeck] wanted me to okay it, and though it makes me out to be a very romantic figure, and I'll practically have to leave town after publication until things quiet down, still it's a fine job and I approved thoroughly."[3] Steinbeck recalled that after Ed read the draft he told him "Let it go that way. It is written in kindness. Such a thing can't be bad."[4]

At that time, of course, no one in their wildest imagination thought that the plain structure on Ocean View Avenue would provide the location for many of the concepts and ideas later used by one of America's most famous authors.

Unfortunately, on November 25, 1936, a large fire in the adjacent Del Mar Cannery destroyed both the cannery and Ed Ricketts' lab. In fact, the fire spread so rapidly that Ed barely escaped the burning building. He rebuilt his lab in 1937 with funds from fire insurance and with the money received when he sold twenty-five feet of his lot to another Monterey local, Yee King.[5] At this writing, the rebuilt building still exists.

Not long after the lab was rebuilt, Ricketts was drafted into World War II at the age of forty-six, despite the fact that he had already served in World War I. He served as a medical technician at the Presidio in Monterey and was discharged about a year later. During the war, the business activity in the lab almost ended, so Ed worked as a chemist at the Cal-Pac Cannery on Ocean View Avenue, only two and one-half blocks from his office.

In April of 1948, Ed Ricketts began preparation for an exploratory trip to the tidal area of British Columbia. It would provide the final information he needed to complete *The Outer Shores*, the final book in his trilogy that covered the tidal life from the tip of Baja California to British Columbia and the Aleutian Islands. John Steinbeck was set to join him on this trip.

Shortly before Steinbeck left, Ricketts was on his way to the store to get some steaks for dinner at the lab when his car collided with the Del Monte Express, a passenger train. After lingering for three days between life and death, on May 11, 1948, Ed died in the local hospital from the injuries he suffered—a ruptured spleen, punctured lung, and internal bleeding. His son, Ed, Jr., was with him when he passed. According to Steinbeck biographer

1947. Ricketts' library was on the upper floor of the lab.
PAT HATHAWAY PHOTO COLLECTION

The Legacy of the Lab

The lab's special qualities come not from the building itself, but rather from the events that transpired there, and the effects those events had both locally and in the broader community.

After Ed Ricketts' untimely death, the lab was first rented and then sold to a local schoolteacher. Harlan Watkins, who taught both English and science at Monterey High School, rented the vacant lab in the early 1950s for forty dollars a month. He explained to the Yees, who owned the property, that he wanted to be able to bring his literature and science students into Ed's lab, where

1939. These shelves were in the basement of Ricketts' lab.
PAT HATHAWAY PHOTO COLLECTION

2005. The shelves in Ricketts' basement today.

so much science and literature of the modern age had incubated.

Harlan had a group of friends that he invited to join him each Wednesday evening to play favorite jazz records and discuss world politics, philosophy, art, science and, of course, jazz. It was a men-only club. Women were allowed to join in only once a month. Entry to the Lab Group was difficult and a departure was usually permanent. When Jimmy Lyons, a regular guest of the Lab Group, suggested establishing a jazz festival like the East Coast's new Newport festival, the Lab Group members gave his idea their blessing. The result was the creation of the first Monterey Jazz Festival board of directors, and Lyons became its director. The Festival has gone on to become the longest continuously presented jazz festival in the world.

In 1956 Ed Haver and a group of fifteen men purchased the lab from Harlan Watkins for use by the Lab Group. In 1993, the surviving members sold the lab to the City of Monterey for $170,000 in a sort of living trust to ensure it would stay in public hands. In the intervening years, Ricketts' lab has survived as the last bastion of male chauvinism on the shores of Bohemia, and will now, thanks to the character of its members, be preserved in perpetuity for those who fervently cherish being in this sacristy of the Old Row.

In 1983 the Cannery Row Foundation held its first board meeting in the lab. The Foundation was formed to preserve and celebrate the history of Steinbeck's literature and Ed Ricketts' ecological legacy of Cannery Row. Before the end of the 1980s, the Foundation produced five annual Great Cannery Row Reunions, locating and celebrating the lives and times of the many men and women who worked the canneries of the Old Row, and the skippers and fisherman

1946. The exterior of Ricketts' lab has changed little since the 1930s.
PAT HATHAWAY PHOTO COLLECTION

of the fleet that delivered the "silver tide" to old Ocean View Avenue sardine factories. With the formation of the Foundation came a more permanent structure for preservation activities, research, education and, of course, cele-

bration. Several members of the Lab Group were on the charter board of directors. The special relationship the Cannery Row Foundation has had with the Pacific Biological Lab has enabled it to open the lab to the public on Steinbeck's birthday, and in early August as part of the National Steinbeck Center's annual Steinbeck Festival. The members of the Cannery Row Foundation sponsor the majority of events on the Row that herald its history.

2005. Ricketts' lab after the City of Monterey carefully restored the building.

Jackson J. Benson, when the news of Ed's injuries reached Steinbeck in New York City, he said, "The greatest man in the world is dying and there is nothing I can do." Due to travel delays, he reached Monterey only after Ed's death.

When Ed Ricketts died, so did part of the essence of Cannery Row. It is

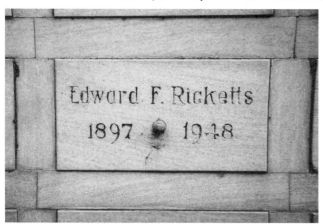

difficult to imagine that any single person who lived there could create as much goodwill. In his study of marine biology, he accumulated considerable research information on the tidal areas along the

2006. Ed Ricketts' ashes are interred in the El Encinal Cemetery.

Pacific Coast. In his personal relationships Ed was always helpful and kind to those who approached him. Indeed, as Audry Lynch wrote in her book, *Steinbeck Remembered,* "Doc was a warm guy who everybody loved. He was a fantastic listener who loved philosophical ideas. He was a first-rate scientist with an imagination backed by an Einstein-type mind." Ed Ricketts was truly an extraordinary man.

A very simple memorial service was held for him at the Little Chapel by the Sea, which is in the "pretty little cemetery" near the "great tide pool" at Point Piños in Pacific Grove. Both locations are prominently featured in Steinbeck's novel. As fate would have it, the people John Steinbeck used as models for his main characters in *Cannery Row,* Ed Ricketts, Flora Woods Domenech Adams and Gabe Bicknell all are close together in El Encinal, the Monterey city cemetery—as close as they were in real life on the Row.

Steinbeck and Ricketts had the habit of playing pranks on each other. However, after his death, Ed may have had the last laugh. A short time after Ed's memorial service, Steinbeck and their pal George Robinson were going through Ed's belongings in the lab. As usual, the safe was open, but it contained a locked compartment. Upon opening it, they found a small bottle of Haig & Haig Scotch whisky and a note that read, "What the hell did you expect to find in here? Here's a drink for your troubles."[6]

The unique relationship between Steinbeck and Ricketts is summarized very well in this poem by Michael Hemp, founder of the Cannery Row Foundation.

Looking into the mind
and soul of Ed Ricketts,
John Steinbeck found answers for his questions,
meaning for his words,
understanding he could not reach alone.
The Row still keeps its mute vigil
For the unthanked genius
of Ed Ricketts

Late 1930s.
In this, the only
known photo of
Flora Woods, a
careful examination
of her hair reveals
that she was
wearing one of
her famous wigs.
PAT HATHAWAY
PHOTO COLLECTION

Dora is a great woman, a great big woman with flaming orange hair
and a taste for Nile green evening dresses.

—CHAPTER THREE

CHAPTER 2

FLORA WOODS AND HER LONE STAR CAFÉ

STEINBECK'S DORA FLOOD WAS BASED ON FLORA WOODS, a madam and a dedicated philanthropist in Monterey during the years Steinbeck lived there. Dora's character very accurately portrayed the way Flora conducted herself and her business in Monterey.

Flora was born Julia Silva in Carmel Valley, California, on April 9, 1876. For whatever reason, Julia changed her name to Flora, a shortened version of Florinda, her mother's name. The 1880 U.S. Census for the outlying area of Monterey lists several Silva families; however, only one family had a daughter age four, the age little Julia would have been in 1880. The same U.S. Census listed her father, Estulan, as a laborer, not as a ship's captain as local legend states. The Silva family was of Portuguese extraction.

As a Carmel Valley native, Flora probably attended the Little Red Schoolhouse, still located on Highway 1, just south of Carmel. She grew to be a large woman, around six feet tall and well over two hundred pounds. Flora's grandson recalled that reports of the color of Flora's wigs varied from red to orange, depending on who saw her. Steinbeck later told his son Thom that Flora wore wigs to cover areas on her head where she had lost considerable amounts of hair. Flora's skin problem was due to occasional outbreaks of scabies, which causes itching and loss of hair. Thom noted that Ricketts treated her with a cream that was used for dogs with mange, which has the same symptoms.

On May 31, 1895, Flora married Charles Woods, a highly regarded cowboy in Monterey. Woods was a California native, a fact that dispels the long-held local legend that her most famous establishment, the Lone Star Café, was so named because her first husband was a cowboy from Texas. They had a son, but nothing is known about him.[7] Their marriage ended sadly when Flora left Woods over his excessive drinking and physical abuse. He committed suicide several months later, on November 20, 1896, in the old Union Saloon on Monterey's Pearl Street.

Little is known about Flora's whereabouts for a number of years after her husband's death. In a 1935 newspaper article, Nettie, one of Flora's two daughters from an unknown liaison, stated that she and her mother lived in Watsonville in the very early 1900s. They then moved to Monterey and lived above the Club Saloon at 403 Alvarado Street. During this time, Flora had "four or five stepfathers" for Nettie and her sister, Ida.[8]

By 1911, Flora and Nettie lived at 520 Prescott Street in Monterey.[9] In 1916, Flora operated a tamale parlor at 431 Lighthouse Avenue. According to Jimmy Rodriquez, a local policeman, it is very likely that those tamales were only a front for one of Flora's earliest brothels.

Sparky Enea, a longtime resident of Monterey, stated that Flora had a large green house on Decatur Street, a brothel that opened around 1918.[10] Her home was listed at 309 Decatur Street in the 1923 *Polk Directory*. The building's owner, accompanied by the police chief, evicted her from her Decatur Street place during that same year.[11] In the meantime, Flora had married Santiago Domenech on September 9, 1919.[12] She divorced him on October 1, 1923, on grounds of cruelty, asserting that he had stolen money from her and had beaten her.[13]

ca.1925. This view shows the Lone Star Café building. Flora added the visible second story prior to opening as a brothel. The building in the foreground is the Wing Chong Co.(Lee Chong's) and the open space beyond it is the vacant lot.

PAT HATHAWAY PHOTO COLLECTION

After being evicted from Decatur Street, Flora moved her ladies to the Lone Star Café, but it is not clear when Flora actually opened for business in that building. The Chinese Joss House, an important religious shrine, was located just behind the building Flora chose, and the Wing Chong Co. was just down the street. It is certain that she was in operation by 1926, since the 1926 *Polk Directory* listed the Lone Star's address as 735 Ocean View Avenue and identified its owner and business as "Mrs. Flora Woods, furnished rooms."

The new brothel was located at 799 Ocean View Avenue, in a building formerly used as a Chinese restaurant. In the mid-1920s, the western portion of Ocean View Avenue where 799 was located contained canneries, and a fairly large Chinese population lived there. The Chinese restaurant was then called the Lone Star Café. Florus Williams recalled that in keeping with the Texas theme of its name, the café had a large five-pointed star on the front of the building, but why a Chinese café was named after Texas' nickname has been lost to history.

Although many have argued otherwise, Flora could not have moved directly from her home on Decatur Street into the Lone Star Café building, since the new location would have required extensive remodeling before it could be a well-appointed brothel. The conversion included adding a second story, according to her grandson Dick Shaw and area resident Irene Longueira. During the renovation period and her early years of operation, Flora either rented or leased the building before she bought it on March 7, 1928.[14] Monterey County property records show that Flora also bought and sold many other properties during her career in Monterey. She frequently used them as collateral for loans of $5,000 to $7,500.

> *But on the left-hand boundary of the [vacant] lot is the stern and stately whorehouse of Dora Flood . . ."* —CHAPTER THREE

In his 1951 essay, "About Ed Ricketts," Steinbeck describes Flora as "a large-hearted woman and a law-abiding citizen in every way except one— she did violate the nebulous laws against prostitution. But since the police didn't seem to care, she felt all right about it and even made little presents in various directions." Many Cannery Row residents, including Dottie Bicknell Sanchez, recall that Steinbeck described his friend Flora in similar terms.

Information regarding the Lone Star Café would have gone unknown to

1939. Flora's Lone Star Café (Dora's Bear Flag Restaurant) is shown at 799 Ocean View Avenue (Cannery Row). On the right, the vacant lot is partly visible and the roof of Ed Ricketts' lab is at the bottom left.

PAT HATHAWAY PHOTO COLLECTION

1996. Irene Longueira came from Spain in 1920 and joined her family on Ocean View Avenue (Cannery Row).

this day had it not been revealed by an eyewitness, Irene Longueira, who moved from Spain in 1920 to join her family. They lived on Ocean View Avenue, not far from the Lone Star. Irene recalled that in 1922, she had gone into the café when it was still a Chinese restaurant with four workers' shacks behind it.

Irene said that while Flora owned the brothel, locals usually called it Flora's, not the Lone Star Café. Flora's manner in running her establishment earned it the title of the best brothel in Monterey. To earn and keep the title meant that the place was nicely decorated, clean, prices were fair, and no trouble of any kind was tolerated, noted former Row policeman Jimmy Rodriquez, who had many opportunities to observe the activities at Flora's. Just as *Cannery Row* suggests that Doc and Dora were close, Ed Ricketts was a good friend of Flora Woods. Both Ricketts and Steinbeck would go into Flora's, individually or together, to have a beer and talk to the girls. Neither man had any other type of relationship with the girls.[15]

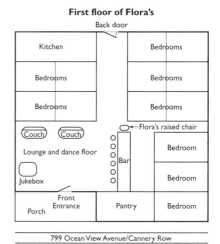

First floor of Flora's

799 Ocean View Avenue/Cannery Row

BASED ON A DRAWING MADE BY JIMMY RODRIQUEZ, APRIL 20, 1996

Upon entering Flora's from the front door on Ocean View Avenue, visitors first encountered a long bar which had a large chair at one end, a chair that was raised off the floor on a wooden platform. From this seat, Flora had a commanding view of the bar and the large lounge area that adjoined it. The lounge contained a jukebox, couches and a dance floor. Here the girls greeted their customers prior to adjourning to the back rooms. The rear area also contained a kitchen where the cook prepared meals for the girls.[16]

In addition to the front door, according to Rodriquez, Flora's place had a rear entrance for men who did not want to risk being seen entering the brothel from Ocean View Avenue.

. . . and the city officials and prominent businessmen who came in the rear entrance back by the railroad tracks. —CHAPTER SIXTEEN

Gabe Bicknell's daughter, Dottie Bicknell Sanchez, recalled that "When us kids were near the back door of Flora's, the men would give us coins so we would not say we saw them."[17] She said she knew the name of one of the men who gave her coins, because at the time, he was a well-known one-armed judge in Monterey. "There was a back door to Flora's that men who were mar-

2005. Flora Woods once owned this house at Laine and David Streets in New Monterey.

ried used because they did not want to be seen using the front door," concurred Monterey local Irene Longueira.

Owning the most successful brothel in Monterey was bound to draw some negative attention. In Flora's case it came from a local newspaper, the *Monterey Trader*. For reasons that have not been substantiated, the newspaper decided to make trouble for Flora by publishing the license plate numbers and photos of her customers, a tactic called "Winchelling" after the popular radio gossipmonger of the era, Walter Winchell.[18]

Despite her unpopularity with some local residents, other people on the Row loved Flora for her overwhelming generosity. Throughout Monterey, Flora Woods Domenech was widely known for her large and continuous acts of charity on behalf of the poor residents of the community, actions Steinbeck captured in Dora's character.

Dora saw the hungry children of Cannery Row and the jobless fathers and the worried women and Dora paid grocery bills right and left for two years and very nearly went broke in the process. —CHAPTER THREE

Florus Williams, the younger brother of gas-station proprietor Red Williams, recalled that in the 1930s his wife worked at J.C. Penney in Monterey and observed that Flora would come in and buy toys and clothes, then distribute them to needy families.

*Dora, who was soft as a mouse's belly, could be as hard as carborundum. She went back
to the Bear Flag and organized it for service [during the influenza epidemic] . . .
The girls kept up with their business but they went in shifts to sit with the families,
and they carried pots of soup when they went.* —CHAPTER SIXTEEN

One of Flora's girls recalled years later that, "At Flora's request I placed a huge order at Wing Chong's for holiday gifts and Flora said she'd kill Mr. Yee if he told people who paid for it."[19] Sparky Enea explained that on Thanksgiving and Christmas, Flora, working from her list of poor families, would hire a taxi to deliver food and gifts.[20] Dottie Bicknell Sanchez added that, "Flora lived on the first floor. My mother, who was a good friend of Flora, took me there several times to see her. Because I liked music, Flora offered to buy me a violin. That was the way she was, always helping people."

In addition to providing gifts and food to poor families, Flora's selflessness seemed to have no limits. Consider the Manaka story:

The large Manaka family lived in a small house on Franklin Street next to Flora's other brothel, the Golden Stairs. Mrs. Manaka was extremely ill, and her husband was very concerned about the extremely loud noises emanating from the Golden Stairs, noise so loud that his poor wife couldn't sleep at night. Aware of Flora's great generosity toward poor people, Frank Manaka did not take the matter to the police, but instead went to see her and explained the situation. Flora knew the family had ten children so she said, "I have a large house in Seaside at 190 Williams Street—go out and see if you like it."

1999. Flora Woods owned this house at 190 Williams Street in Seaside. In 1936, she made it possible for the Manaka family to buy it.

According to Manaka's son, who remembered the incident, Frank looked at the large house, and told Flora he liked it. As a result, on May 26, 1936, Flora traded them her large house for their small house plus a very small monthly payment.[21] Flora neither sought nor wanted any credit for her many charitable acts—just like Steinbeck's Dora.

In the 1930s, the going rate for the customers at Flora's was two dollars. Because many of her customers were fishermen, if the fishing was bad, Flora extended credit for services rendered. Dick Shaw, Flora's grandson, shared an interesting exchange he had with her in the late 1930s. Dick worked in the canneries and he had not yet met his famous grandmother. One day he discovered that he needed a small amount of money to get by until the next payday, so he went into Flora's and introduced himself. Even though they were related, the family was separated and Dick's parents weren't on good terms with Flora most of the time. Flora was surprised at the seventeen-year old boy's audacity at marching into a brothel in the middle of the day. Dick recalled that she was taken aback by his introduction and more so when he asked to borrow two dollars. Dick did not know that two dollars was the going rate at Flora's. When she heard he wanted two dollars, she naturally thought he wanted to spend it on a girl. Flora told him he could not spend the money in her place and that she would charge him interest on the loan. At the mention of an interest charge, Dick left and did not see her again until shortly before her death.

The long and highly successful run of Flora's Lone Star Café came to an end on June 2, 1941, when California's attorney general, Earl Warren, ordered all the brothels in the state closed. Ed Ricketts wrote Sparky Enea in

2005. This concrete building stands on the land that Flora's Lone Star Café once occupied.

1942, "You probably heard the sad story of the Lone Star (brothel). Everything was moved out, including, of course, all the beds—and, boy, were there a lot of them."[22] Because she no longer had use for the building, Flora sold the house and the land on August 27, 1942, to Victor and Virginia Ferrante. The Ferrantes immediately sold it to Monterey Fish Products. In the mid-1940s, the owners of Monterey Fish Products tore down the wooden building that had served Flora and her customers so well, and built the concrete structure that still stands. Over the years, the building changed ownership several times. At the time of this writing it housed Mackerel Jack's, a tourist store.

Shortly after the Lone Star Café closed, Flora married for a third time, on November 6, 1941, to Earl "Tiny" Adams.[23] Adams owned Orange Cab Company, a taxi firm whose main source of business had been taking customers to and from Flora's. Consequently, it is not unreasonable to assume that Adams named his Orange Cab Company after Flora's famous orange wigs, opined Jimmy Rodriquez. Flora and Tiny eventually moved into a second-story apartment at 360 Alvarado Street.

1995. The gravestone of Flora Woods Domenech Adams in Monterey's El Encinal Cemetery.

Flora suffered from increasingly poor health, and passed away from a heart attack on August 1, 1948.[24] Despite her profession, possibly the best summary of Flora Woods Domenech Adams is the following statement by Ed Ricketts: "She is one hell of a woman. I wish good people could be so good."[25]

Some of the pallbearers at Flora's funeral seemed to have stepped out of *Cannery Row*. They included fisherman Sparky Enea, bar owner Jimmy Brucia and Johnny Garcia, an entertainer who worked at Jimmy's.[26] Flora was buried in the Monterey cemetery on Fremont Street. Thus ended the life and career of one of Monterey's best-known citizens and the model for a major character in both Steinbeck's *Cannery Row* and *Sweet Thursday*.

> *Now there is one hell of a woman. No wonder she got to be a madam.*
> *There is one hell of a woman.* —CHAPTER TWENTY-THREE

ca. 1930s. Won Yee standing
beside a truck loaded with
bundled dried squid.
MONTEREY PUBLIC LIBRARY,
CALIFORNIA HISTORY ROOM ARCHIVES

Lee was round faced and courteous. He spoke a stately English without ever using the letter R....[his] mouth was full and benevolent and the flash of gold when he smiled was rich and warm.

—CHAPTER ONE

CHAPTER 3

WON YEE AND WING CHONG CO.

STEINBECK PRIMARILY BASED THE CHARACTER LEE CHONG on Monterey local Won Yee and, to a lesser extent, his son Jack Yee. Won Yee immigrated from China to San Francisco in 1900.[27] After spending a number of years in San Francisco, he moved to Monterey in 1918 and, with several partners, opened the Wing Chong Co. Won Yee's wife, daughter and son left China and joined him in Monterey in the same year.[28]

Steinbeck rarely used a person's real name in the book. Instead, he would create one better suited to a particular character. In the case of Lee Chong,

Steinbeck may have borrowed the name from a prominent Chinese business-man who was one of the founders of the Monterey Fish Canning Company. Perhaps he wanted to connect Won Yee with another successful Chinese American.

Lee Chong's grocery, while not a model of neatness,
was a miracle of supply. —CHAPTER ONE

Because his is the only name associated with the store, many people assume Won Yee was the owner, but he could not have been. At the time Chinese immigrants could not own property; Won Yee leased the land from King Fook Wing of San Francisco, who was a citizen and therefore could own property The lease was for twenty-five years at ninety dollars a year.[29]

At the time of the book's setting, the late 1930s, the store existed exactly where Steinbeck placed it, at 835 Ocean View Avenue. In keeping with the custom among many Chinese businessmen, Won Yee gave his store a grand name—Wing Chong, which means "glorious successful."[30] Over the years,

1947. This view of a front window of the Wing Chong Co. is very similar to that in the 1930s.
PAT HATHAWAY PHOTO COLLECTION

the store certainly lived up to its name. Steinbeck simply changed the name from the Wing Chong Co. to "Lee Chong's."

From his early days in Cannery Row, Won Yee was an enterprising and successful businessman. In addition to effectively managing the Wing Chong Co., Won Yee was involved in trade and real-estate transactions near the store.

In 1924, Won Yee recognized that there was still a strong demand for dried squid in China. To fill the need, he bought squid from Chinese and Italian fishermen. Because of the offensive odor of drying squid, Monterey passed a law forbidding that activity within city limits. Won Yee leased land outside the city across from the airport, in an area called Tarpey Flats. To make the process more efficient, Won Yee invented a machine that cleaned and compressed the squid for transport to market. Because of his vision and

ca. 1940s. This photo shows the counter that Lee Chong used in the *Cannery Row*. The clerk is Sam Chan, a longtime employee of the Yee family.

abilities, in 1932 he shipped ten thousand tons of dried squid to Hong Kong with an estimated value of $50,000 to $80,000—a very significant sum during the Depression.[31]

Won Yee was highly regarded by his customers. While he was known to be a shrewd businessman, Dottie Bicknell Sanchez recalled that he never hesitated to extend credit to the cannery workers' families so they would have food between paychecks.

A two-story wooden building that housed his Wing Chong Co. still stands. The second story has an outdoor porch that extends the width of the building. The Yee family and any relatives lived in the front area of the second floor just off the porch. The rest of the second floor consisted of a hallway with rooms that

ca. late 1950s. The Wing Chong Co. after the Yee family closed the store due to drastically reduced cannery operations.

PAT HATHAWAY PHOTO COLLECTION

Rumors and Mysteries

Rumors have persisted that the Wing Chong Co. building contained secret passageways to the outside and into the La Ida, another brothel that was adjacent to the west. The passages were to be used as escape routes when the police raided the building for opium users. The rumored passageways proved to be real, and opium users escaped through them during police raids in the 1920s and early 1930s.

A large mural of a wolf in one of Wing Chong's second-floor rental rooms has also created a great deal of curiosity over the years, as people either saw the work or discovered it through rumor. Because the *Lone Wolf* was dated 1935, most people assumed that a renter had painted it in the 1930s. However, Francis Yee, the widow of Won Yee's son Jack, stated that

1986. *The Lone Wolf* in an upstairs room at the Wing Chong Co.
MICHAEL K. HEMP

when she and her family lived there from the mid-1930s to the mid-1950s, no painting existed. She can be certain of that because the room in question was in the Yee family area on the second floor and, had there been a painting, she would have seen it. Monterey resident Bill Johnk, the master craftsman who constructed a scale model of Cannery Row, lived in one of the second floor rented rooms in 1966 and he recalls having seen the painting. Johnk figures that the *Lone Wolf* was painted between the time the Yees left the building in the mid-1950s and 1966. One can safely assume, then, that the anonymous painter purposely misdated his mural, attempting to "place" the piece during the years of Steinbeck's *Cannery Row*.

were rented to local workers. In fact, the 1930 U.S. Census lists thirteen renters, all Chinese workers.

> The grocery store occupied the first floor. The large room was very well organized and contained all the standard brand-name groceries, as well as dried lychee nuts, Chinese tea and frozen squid for bait. Hunting and fishing licenses were available along with the necessary equipment. Wing Chong also sold men's work clothes, surf waders, fountain pens, cigarettes, lighters, Bull Durham tobacco, beer and whiskey."[32] The market even had a special beer, the True Blue Brand.[33]

. . . within its single room a man could find everything he needed or wanted to live and be happy. —CHAPTER ONE

From the day the store opened in 1918, the Wing Chong Co. supplied the needs of the inhabitants of Cannery Row in many diverse ways. Cannery workers bought their work clothes there, kids got candy, Ed Ricketts bought his beer from the store's icebox (the glass-doored icebox still stands in the Wing Chong building at 835 Cannery Row, and Steinbeck enthusiasts can stand before it, exactly where Ed did.) In general, it is safe to say that anyone who needed just about anything could find it at the Wing Chong Co. In addition, the Wing Chong Co. had a small restaurant at the west end of the building.

1986. The icebox at the Wing Chong Co. (Lee Chong's) where Ed (Doc) got his beer. You can stand today where Ed stood then.
MICHAEL K. HEMP

Lee wouldn't look at him as he got two quarts of beer out of the icebox. —CHAPTER TWENTY-ONE

2005. The Wing Chong Co. building. The Yee Family lived in rooms just behind the second floor porch.

When Won Yee died in 1934, his son Jack continued to operate the store until it closed in the mid-1950s. When the canneries were no longer financially viable, the same was true of the Wing Chong Co. and the Yee family closed it. At this writing, the space that once was occupied by the Wing Chong grocery store holds a variety store.

498

Mack was the elder, leader, mentor, and to a small extent, the exploiter
of a little group of men who had in common no families, no money,
and no ambitions beyond food, drink and contentment.
—CHAPTER ONE

CHAPTER 4

GABE BICKNELL AND THE PALACE

WHILE MACK IS A FICTITIOUS CHARACTER, HE WAS BASED ON a very good friend of John Steinbeck named Harold "Gabe" Bicknell. After *Cannery Row* was published in 1945, Steinbeck wrote his editor, Pat Covici, that "Gabe, who is my Mack, came to me quite drunk today."[34] In addition to Mack, Steinbeck used some aspects of Bicknell's life to create Gay, who was "one of the boys."

Harold Otis "Gabe" Bicknell, born on February 7, 1904, in New Castle, Indiana, was the son of Carl and Bessie Bicknell. The family consisted of

1921. Harold "Gabe" Bicknell during his enlistment in the army.
DOTTIE BICKNELL SANCHEZ COLLECTION

Gabe, his brother Cecil and sister Lucille. Not much is known about his early years, but from family photographs it appears that as a boy Bicknell liked horses and the activities typical of young boys. Photographs also indicate that he once played for a semi-professional baseball team. Bicknell enlisted in the U.S. Army December 17, 1920 and was honorably discharged on July 13, 1921. He returned to New Castle, where he worked as a laborer. There is very little information on Gabe's activities or whereabouts from 1923 to 1928.

For reasons unknown, in 1927 Bicknell left the Midwest and moved to San Jose, where he had relatives. From there, Gabe moved sixteen miles west to the small town of Saratoga and married Dorothy Jasper in nearby Redwood City in 1928. He was employed as a grocery clerk, and Dorothy was a telephone operator.[35] Their first child was born in late 1928 and was named Dorothy. To avoid confusion, little Dorothy was given the nickname of Dottie, which carried into adulthood.

The Bicknell family moved to Monterey in 1929, presumably so Gabe could get work as a mechanic in the canneries. The Bicknells rented a house at 741 Laine Street. A son, Harold, was born in the house on September 7, 1929.[36] Over the next five years, three more daughters were born: Betty, Bessie and Arlene.

From 1929 until his death on December 30, 1954, Gabe Bicknell had a serious

1996. The Bicknell family lived in this house at 214 Alder Street in Pacific Grove in the mid-1930s.

drinking problem. Because of his alcoholism, Gabe had a habit of working for a short period of time and then quitting and going on a drinking binge, his daughter Dottie recalled. Bicknell's long-suffering wife had to call the police numerous times to have him arrested for drunkenness. He spent many days and nights in the Pacific Grove jail, then housed in the building on Forest Avenue that now houses the current city hall. If he was gone for a period of weeks, Dottie's mother would tell her, "We know where Dad is: the county jail in Salinas."

In the early 1930s when the Bicknell family lived in Seaside, a town near Monterey, Dottie suffered a severe case of pneumonia. Their rented house was leaky and in bad repair. Proving what a good friend he was to Gabe,

Early 1920s. Harold "Gabe" Bicknell with his father Carl at their home in New Castle, Indiana.
DOTTIE BICKNELL SANCHEZ COLLECTION

Steinbeck moved the Bicknells into his maternal grandmother's house at Second Street and Central Avenue in Pacific Grove, where they remained until Dottie recovered. After the oldest daughter regained her health, the family lived in many different rented houses in Pacific Grove. On many occasions Steinbeck would bring the family a large amount of fish he had caught, and Dorothy would cook for Steinbeck and the family.

Tired of his excessive drinking, Dorothy divorced Gabe Bicknell on June 26, 1936, citing "intemperance" as grounds.[37] Dottie remembered with emotion that, "We really missed seeing him, but he did not want us to see him drunk, and our mother would not let him in the house if he had been drinking." To visit with their father, Dottie and her siblings would go to Red

Williams' service station on Lighthouse Avenue in Pacific Grove when their dad and Steinbeck were there. During such visits, it was not unusual for Steinbeck to give the kids coins to go to the movies. Dottie recalled that for as long as she could remember Steinbeck and her father were very good friends, although she never knew how they became such good friends—only that they were.

1935. Gabe Bicknell's work record at Won Yee's squid-drying fields outside of Monterey.

Few people ever realized that Steinbeck had such a close relationship with Bicknell and his family dating back to the early 1930s. When Steinbeck left Monterey for New York City, he and Gabe corresponded regularly. The following paragraph comes from a letter Steinbeck wrote to Gabe in 1953. Its content confirms that their friendship was much more than a casual one. In this letter, Steinbeck referred to *Sweet Thursday,* his second book about Cannery Row.

> I have just finished another book about The Row. It is a continuation concerned not with what happened, but with what might have happened. The one can be as true as the other. As a book, this will probably be out next summer or fall. Then Rodgers and Hammerstein are making a play with music of it for late fall or early spring. This should be fun. I think it is a funny story—and sad too because it is what might have happened to Ed and didn't. I don't seem to be able to get over his death. But this will be the last piece about him. Did you ever see the little biography I wrote about him for the second edition of *The Sea of Cortez?*"[38]

In addition to providing Steinbeck with the material to create Mack and Gay, Gabe was also the source of other useful material, such as "Oh, hooptedoodle," a phrase that Dottie said her dad often uttered. Steinbeck may have

1945. Gabe Bicknell stands on Wave Street with the Palace behind him.

PETER STACKPOLE, MARTHA HEASLEY COX CENTER FOR STEINBECK STUDIES, SAN JOSE STATE UNIVERSITY

used these words in *Sweet Thursday* after having learned them from Gabe.

Gabe and Steinbeck often played pranks on each other. Dottie recalled the time that her dad and his friends sent a tightly wrapped package of smelly fishmeal to Steinbeck at his home in New York. After Gabe had spoken to Steinbeck and found out that he had received the package, he told Dottie, "He got it; now we have to wait and find out what he will do to us." Such retaliation was all in the spirit of playful friendship.

Regardless of his wayward ways, Bicknell did the best he could to provide for his family. Despite his problems with alcohol, he could always get work in the canneries because he was an excellent mechanic.[39] In addition to working periodically in the canneries, Gabe earned money by collecting specimens for Ed Ricketts, working at Won Yee's squid-drying business, and collecting golf balls. His family got their food at Won Yee's Wing Chong Co. because they could get credit, and Dottie recalled that her dad would pay the

1939. The rusty pipes and other discarded cannery items are clearly visible on the "vacant lot."
PAT HATHAWAY PHOTO COLLECTION

bill when he worked. Even after the divorce, Gabe continued to provide for his family when he could, she said.

Mack and the boys . . . are the Virtues, the Graces, the Beauties of the hurried mangled craziness of Monterey —CHAPTER TWO

While on a drinking binge, Bicknell could usually be found with his crew of "bums" around the "Palace Flophouse" or the old vacant lot. The vacant lot was located almost directly across from Ed's lab on Ocean View Avenue, where Steinbeck placed it in the book. The lot contained many different types of rusty pipes of all sizes, boilers and anything else that had out-

2005. The "vacant lot." It is far more vacant than in the 1930s, when it actually housed discarded cannery equipment. This photo was taken from the steps of Ricketts' lab.

lived its usefulness at the canneries. The lot and the pipes provided a convenient place for the bums to gather, share a bottle of wine, and discuss the
affairs of the day. Though the vacant lot was certainly not vacant, its name
originated in the 1920s before the canneries developed.

*The bums who retired in disgust under the black cypress tree came out to sit on
the rusty pipes in the vacant lot.* —CANNERY ROW

The large black cypress on the lot was thriving during the mid-1930s. It
was located on the
slightly elevated
part at the rear of
the vacant lot. The
black cypress had
very long, low,
overhanging
branches that pro-
vided a convenient
place for the bums
to take a break and
relax. Row resident
Irene Longueira
remembered that

1940s. Harold "Gabe" Bicknell poses on a cannery building with a fish
hopper and Monterey Bay in the background.
DOTTIE BICKNELL SANCHEZ COLLECTION

the tree was ordered cut down in the early 1940s, by Manuel Perry,
Monterey's superintendent of streets. *Cannery Row* enthusiasts sometimes mistake the cypress tree on the top of Bruce Ariss Way on Wave Street for the
one in the book. That tree was located behind the rooming house that was
known in the book as "the Palace."

The bums, as Steinbeck called them, were male alcoholics who hung out
under the black cypress tree, sat on the rusty pipes in the vacant lot and
stayed in the local flophouses. According to Jimmy Rodriquez, who policed
the Cannery Row beat from 1937 to 1942, the bums often sat on the pipes
in the lot drinking wine, but did not bother anyone. Most of the men
Steinbeck characterized as bums were generally full-time drinkers who had
occasional bouts of employment. They worked at various jobs in the canner-

1945. The two-story apartment building that inspired the Palace Flophouse and Grill in *Cannery Row*.
PETER STACKPOLE, MARTHA HEASLEY COX CENTER FOR STEINBECK STUDIES, SAN JOSE STATE UNIVERSITY

ies, collected golf balls, served as caddies, and did general labor; several were periodically employed by Ed Ricketts to collect frogs, butterflies, cats and tide pool life.

At certain times when large sardine catches were landed, extra cannery workers were needed in a hurry. Someone from the canneries would go over to the vacant lot and wake up a few of these homeless locals to get them to work. One cannery worker confessed that the men often smelled so bad that the cannery personnel preferred to wake them with a nudge of their foot rather than touch them.[40]

Because of their aversion to steady employment and the regular income it provided, the homeless needed an inexpensive source of alcohol. Fortunately for them, in the mid-1930s, a gallon of less-than-the-best red wine cost thirty-nine cents.[41]

The men would sometimes spend the night in the area's various flophouses, which included the rooms above the Wing Chong Co. and the Ocean View Hotel at 403 Ocean View Avenue, as well as various small shacks in the area. Longtime cannery worker and Row resident Charlie Nonella commented on the Ocean View Hotel, "You could rent a room for seventy-five cents a night, and the sheets were still warm."[42] The Palace Flophouse and Grill was Mack's favorite stopover.

Mack and the boys loved the Palace and they even cleaned it a little sometimes. In their minds they sneered at unsettled people who had no house to go to and occasionally in their pride they brought a guest home for a day or two. —CHAPTER SEVEN

The Palace Flophouse and Grill building was based on a real place, but its origin in the book was much different than in reality. To create the Palace building in the book, Steinbeck used a nearby fishmeal warehouse called Minnick's.[43] It was located westward in the 800 block of Wave Street, but in the book Steinbeck moved it to the real location of the Palace, which was 798 Wave Street. Steinbeck may have invented the name of the Palace Flophouse and Grill by slightly changing and combining the names of two establishments that had been located on Alvarado Street in Monterey—the Palace Hotel and the Palace Grill.

Steinbeck created a fictional owner, Horace Abbeville, who sold the building to Lee Chong (based on Won Yee) who then allowed Mack and the boys to move in. The reality of the Palace ownership was that on September 23, 1927, Won Yee leased the land from King Fook Wing of San Francisco for twenty-five years at ten dollars a year rent.[44] The actual building at 798 Wave Street was erected about 1931. Irene Longueira said it was owned by Won Yee and John Dana, a local insurance agent who had considerable real-estate holdings within Monterey. The building had three or four apartments that were rented out, and Gabe used the building as his address during one of his brief stays in 1949.

2005. In the 1950s, Harold "Gabe" Bicknell lived in this apartment building at 425 Ocean View Avenue. He died as the result of injuries he suffered in a fire here.

Remembering Gabe

Despite Gabe's frequent alcohol-induced antics, he was thought of as a good person, a very capable mechanic and, when he was sober, a loving father. The following comments are from people who knew him on Cannery Row:

CHARLIE NONELLA, a friend of Gabe and a cannery worker, stated, "He was a very good maintenance and construction man, specializing in the mechanical parts of the conveyor lines."

JIMMY RODRIQUEZ, the policeman on the Cannery Row beat, had many occa-

2005. Gabe's oldest daughter, Dottie Bicknell Sanchez.

sions to see Gabe and recalled, "I knew Gabe well. Overall, despite his drinking problems, he was a nice and kind man."

ELENA YOUNG recalled that on Sundays if it was almost dark, Gabe and his pals would make certain that she, a friend and her brother got home safely from the movies.

DOTTIE BICKNELL SANCHEZ fondly remembered, "Dad, when he wasn't drinking, was fun to be around. He was funny, kind, and he was also a good ventriloquist."

The wooden building had two stories and a corrugated steel roof. Irene Longueira, who lived next door, observed that it had four or five apartments and was mainly inhabited by Chinese workers prior to World War II. In order to enhance the story, Steinbeck changed the Palace's interior from apartments to a large room that Mack and the boys lived in with their large stove. The building continued to be inhabited as an apartment building until the early 1970s. Gabe Bicknell gave its address, 798 Wave Street, as his address in 1949.[45] The building was torn down in 1972. The original location can be viewed from Wave Street near the top of Bruce Ariss Way.

Gabe lived or flopped in many different places before and after his divorce. He would stay in various other flophouses, such as the second floor of the Wing Chong Co., or Crespo's on Ocean View Avenue, or rent one of the many one- or two-room shacks available in the Cannery Row area. One very small house he inhabited is still at 498 Wave Street, only slightly changed from 1945. That year, *Life Magazine* photographer Peter Stackpole was sent to Cannery Row to document scenes from Steinbeck's popular novel, and photographed Gabe sitting on the front steps of the Wave Street house. That photograph later appeared on the cover of the 1994 Viking Press edition of *Cannery Row.*

Dottie Bicknell Sanchez vividly recalled the evening of December 11, 1954, when a fire started in Gabe's downstairs apartment. He called her to tell her of the fire and that he was trying to wake up Mrs. Effie Reece, who was in an upstairs apartment. After Gabe made sure she was up, he went back to his apartment to try to get his belongings out. Gabe was

1998. The grave of Harold Otis "Gabe" Bicknell in the Monterey city cemetery, El Encinal.

overcome by smoke and was severely burned. He died from his injuries on December 30, 1954 in the Salinas Hospital,[46] and was buried in the Monterey cemetery. For Harold "Gabe" Bicknell, the road from New Castle, Indiana, to the front cover of *Cannery Row* was indeed a long journey.

In Mack's eyes there was good will and good fellowship and a desire to make everyone happy. —CHAPTER ONE

PART TWO

SECONDARY CHARACTERS AND LOCATIONS

Its inhabitants are, as the man once said, "whores, pimps, gamblers, and sons of bitches," by which he meant "Everybody." Had the man looked through another peephole, he might have said "saints and angels and martyrs and holy men" and he would have meant the same thing.

—CANNERY ROW

pre-1936. Gabe Bicknell (top row, left) and the boys are on a truck located just off Ocean View Avenue (Cannery Row) across from Ricketts' lab. Scenes like this and his knowledge of a specimen-rich Carmel Valley may have given Steinbeck the idea for the great frog-hunting trip.

That is, they lived in the pipes when it was damp but in fine weather they lived in the shadow of the black cypress tree at the top of the lot.

—CHAPTER ONE

CHAPTER 5

ADDITIONAL RESIDENTS

THOUGH MUCH OF *CANNERY ROW*'S PLOT FOCUSES ON ITS four main characters, Steinbeck also included a host of other personalities, both real and invented, to recreate the vibrant world of the Row. Where characters are fictions, or composites, they illustrate the potency of Steinbeck's imagination. Many characters from the novel are purely imaginary, and are listed on page 134. When actual people and places are used, Steinbeck portrays real life on the Row in all its curious complexity.

GAY

It even got as far as the County Jail in Salinas where Gay, who lived the good life by letting the sheriff beat him at checkers, suddenly grew cocky and never lost another game. He lost his privileges that way but he felt like a whole man again. —CHAPTER TWENTY-FIVE

One of "the boys," Gay, was based on Harold "Gabe" Bicknell, who was also Steinbeck's prototype for Mack. When he was sober, Gabe was a very good mechanic; however, when he was drunk—a frequent occurrence—he would try to get back into his house. When this occurred, his wife, Dorothy, would have him arrested and put in jail. Dottie Bicknell Sanchez recalled, "When we lived in Pacific Grove, my mother had him arrested many times for being drunk."

"Take Gay," said Mack. "His old lady hits him."
—CHAPTER THIRTEEN

1945. Gabe, who was a skilled mechanic, is working on a truck engine of a 1941 Nash.
PETER STACKPOLE, MARTHA HEASLEY COX CENTER FOR STEINBECK STUDIES, SAN JOSE STATE UNIVERSITY

On at least one occasion Dorothy was known to have hit Gabe. This usually occurred when Gabe drank too much and, as a result, stepped over Dorothy's rules for her home. One such instance happened in the mid-1930s when the family lived in a small house at 159 Pacific Street in Pacific Grove. Dorothy and her children put their small coins in a jar to save up for a holiday dinner. Dottie remembered that one evening Gabe came in very intoxicated and tried to take the jar. When Dorothy saw what he was trying to do, she hit him with a pot full of hot stew. In addition to his marital problems, Gabe was also involved in tomfoolery around town. In the novel, Gay broke a display window at Holman's Department Store, something Gabe Bicknell did at the real-life department store of the same name.

2005. This was the small house, at 159 Pacific Street in Pacific Grove, where Gabe was hit with a pot of stew by his wife.

Early 1940s. Red Williams' gas station is the oddly-shaped building at the intersection of Lighthouse and Fountain Avenues across from Holman's Department Store.

He was such a wonder, Gay was—the little mechanic of God, the St. Francis of all things that turn and twist and explode, the St. Francis of coils and armatures and gears. And if some time all the heaps of jalopies . . . praise God in a great chorus—it will be largely due to Gay and his brotherhood. —CHAPTER ELEVEN

In the 1930 U.S. Census, Gabe Bicknell's occupation was listed as "mechanic." Florus Williams, whose brother owned the local gas and service station, stated that he frequently saw Gabe tinkering with cars. Dottie recalled that because he was a good mechanic, her dad could always get work in the cannery when he was not drinking.

Bicknell was very aware that, in addition to Mack, he was also the model for Gay. Steinbeck historian Neal Hotelling has seen a copy of *Cannery Row* that Gabe signed "Harold 'Gay' Bicknell." Gabe was not the only one of the "boys" who became part of *Cannery Row*. Two of Gay's friends, the "bums Hughie and

1945. Red Williams pumping gas in his station at the corner of Lighthouse and Fountain Avenues.

PETER STACKPOLE, MARTHA HEASLEY COX CENTER FOR STEINBECK STUDIES, SAN JOSE STATE UNIVERSITY

Jones," collected frogs and cats for the Western Biological Laboratory. Many bums collected specimens for Ed Ricketts—but it's probable that Steinbeck invented the names.

> *. . . Hughie and Jones who occasionally collected frogs and cats*
> *for Western Biological . . .* —CHAPTER ONE

HENRI

> *Henri the painter was not French and his name was not Henri. Also he was not*
> *really a painter. Henri was so steeped in stories of the Left Bank in Paris that he lived*
> *there although he had never been there . . . It is not known whether Henri*
> *was a good painter or not for he threw himself so violently into*
> *movements that he had very little time left for painting*
> *of any kind.* —CHAPTER TWENTY-TWO

People who either knew Steinbeck or those close to him say that his friend, artist Bruce Ariss, was the model for Henri the painter. Ariss and his

2006. The house that Bruce and Jean Ariss inhabited on Lobos Street in the pines above New Monterey.

wife, Jean, lived in the pines above Monterey, in a strangely designed house that Bruce had built, whereas Henri supposedly lived on his boat.

Michael Hemp, the founder of the Cannery Row Foundation, suggests that Robert Henri could be another possible source for the Henri character. Henri was an American painter who lived in New York at the same time as Steinbeck.

THE GIRLS

Probably the busiest time the girls of the Bear Flag ever had was the March of the big sardine catch. It wasn't only that the fish ran in silvery billions but money ran almost as freely. —CHAPTER SIXTEEN

During Flora's busiest period—sardine season—there were usually twelve girls living and working at the Lone Star. Even during the off-season, there were never fewer then five girls employed by the house at one time. Depending on whether or not the fishing season was open, or if there were any conventions in town, there could be ten to twelve girls available. "Available" girls served as back-ups if the "on duty" girl was busy with another customer. At least one girl was always on duty and ready to work no matter what time of day or night.[47]

The girls who worked at the Bear Flag in *Cannery Row* have names such as Eva Flanegan, Phyllis Mae and Elsie Doublebottom. The names, most likely, came from Steinbeck's imagination, but Steinbeck knew some of the girls because he would occasionally stop in to drink a beer and talk with them.[48] Over the years, Flora employed several hundred girls. Many used aliases, and undoubtedly had colorful names. Steinbeck wrote that half the girls were Christian Scientists, but this was not true. John Steinbeck drew on an experience from his own past when he was working in New York City as a reporter in the 1920s. There he met some chorus girls, many of whom were Christian Scientists.[49]

THE WATCHMEN

The watchman [for the Hopkins Marine Station], a dark and surly man, had seen them
and his black cocker spaniel had seen them. He shouted at them and when they didn't
move he came down to the beach . . . "Don't you know you can't lay around here?
*You got to get off. This is private property!" —*CHAPTER FOURTEEN

There was a watchman at the Hopkins Marine Station named Willoughby,
but he was not "dark and surly." He was thought to be a very nice person but,
as indicated in *Cannery Row*, he did have a problem with trespassers.

Ed Ricketts., Jr., recalled that Flora also had a watchman/bouncer on duty
to keep things under control, considering her occupation and clientele. Her
bouncers most often worked in the evening. One of her watchmen was
named Blackie.

OLD CHINAMAN

. . . through the vacant lot came an old Chinaman. He wore an ancient flat straw hat,
blue jeans, both coat and trousers, and heavy shoes of which one sole was loose
*so it slapped the ground when he walked. —*CHAPTER FOUR

There was an older Chinese man whose shoes flapped when he walked
along Cannery Row. Dottie Bicknell Sanchez recalled that she "heard the
Chinese man walking and he made a flap-flap sound like a sole or heel was
loose on his shoes. At that time we lived in one of the three very small houses that were behind Wing Chong's. My dad knew the Chinese man and one
day, when I was sick, the Chinese man brought some Chinese herbs that my
mother made into a tea that made me well. He walked to the beach and we
never saw him again."

BOILER RESIDENTS

. . . great white bells hung down over the boiler door and at night the flowers smelled
of love and excitement, an incredibly sweet and moving odor. —CHAPTER EIGHT

People actually lived in the old boilers on the vacant lot.[50] Only Steinbeck knew if any were really named Malloy. Dottie Bicknell Sanchez remembered "walking by and seeing people who lived in the old boilers. They also cooked there, and they draped towels or blankets over the ends to keep out the weather." By making the large pipes as comfortable as possible, cannery workers could live close to work and save five dollars a month in rent. During the Depression that was a significant savings for a working person. Sleeping in the pipes was a common practice; the authorities were aware of it and gave their tacit approval.

In 1935 Mr. and Mrs. Sam Malloy moved into the boiler . . . Mr. Malloy was happy
there and for quite a long time so was Mrs. Malloy. —CHAPTER EIGHT

1939. Next to the white building are at least two boilers that people like the Malloys lived in.
PAT HATHAWAY PHOTO COLLECTION

ROBERT LOUIS STEVENSON

Monterey is a city with a long and brilliant literary tradition. It remembers with some pleasure and some glory that Robert Louis Stevenson lived there. —CHAPTER TWELVE

Robert Louis Stevenson lived in the Monterey area, but only for four months in 1879. Nonetheless, many people felt that Stevenson's vision of the island in *Treasure Island* developed after his visit to Point Lobos. Several scholars have supported the Point Lobos theory. According to Anne Roller Issler in *Stevenson at Silverado* (Caldwell, Idaho: The Caxton Printers, Ltd., 1939), "Several writers have recognized the Monterey Peninsula and its shoreline here and there in *Treasure Island.*" In an article entitled "Stevenson in Monterey" in the *Pacific Historical Review* (vol. 34, 1965), Issler also mentions that Stevenson and a Chinese man named Tim went on a treasure hunt around Point Lobos. She also claims that Stevenson wrote two articles in the *Monterey Californian* (December 16 and December 23, 1879). Both stories involve treasure hunts.

1930s. This is how the Carmel Valley and Carmel River appeared at the time of the book's setting. Note the orchards in the middle of the photo, just as Steinbeck stated in Chapter Thirteen.

PAT HATHAWAY PHOTO COLLECTION

1939. This aerial view shows the heart of Cannery Row from the Monterey Canning Co. on the left to Hovden's Cannery (Morden's) on the right. Between the two tall smokestacks are Flora's, Ed's lab, the vacant lot, Wing Chong Co., and La Ida.

Historian Roy Nickerson, the author of *Robert Louis Stevenson in California*, believes that Point Lobos inspired *Treasure Island* because the landscape of the island is so similar to the one in the book. He also claims that the Caribbean Islands, which many people believe to be the true setting of *Treasure Island*, have "no sea lions or other such beasts as described, no pines or cypress, and Stevenson himself had never been there." Furthermore, when Stevenson wrote about Monterey in his 1880 book *The Old and New Pacific Capitals*, he described the area in the same tone and style he used for his novel.

FRANKIE

He [Frankie] couldn't learn and there was something a little wrong with his coordination. He wasn't an idiot, he wasn't dangerous, his parent, or parents, wouldn't pay for his keep in an institution . . . Doc clipped Frankie's hair and got rid of the lice. At Lee Chong's he got him a new pair of overalls and a striped sweater and Frankie became his slave. —CHAPTER TEN

Frankie was a young boy who hung around the lab and adored Doc. Over the years, speculators have suggested a number of possibilities for the origins of Frankie's character. Most likely Frankie was based on Frankie Bergara. Michael Hemp recalled that, in the early 1930s, Frankie was a kid who frequented Ed Ricketts' lab and knew Ed well. Frankie Bergara had a learning disability, as did Steinbeck's character.[51]

JOSH BILLINGS

Once the town was greatly outraged over what the citizens considered to be a slight to an author. It had to do with Josh Billings, the great humorist . . . —CHAPTER TWELVE

In the late 1800s, Henry Wheeler Shaw was a well-known humorist who used the pseudonym Josh Billings. Although Billings lived from 1818 to 1885, Steinbeck resurrected him and had him live and die in Monterey in the

1930s. In his real life, Billings began to write humorous sketches and home-spun philosophies in a rural dialect and eventually became a popular speaker. His best humor was published in his annual *Farmer's Allminax* (1869-1880).

THE SINGING BARTENDER

Jimmy Brucia felt it and Johnny his singing bartender. —CHAPTER TWENTY-FIVE

As journalist Bonnie Gartshore noted, Johnny Garcia (1914-1963) worked as a bartender at Jimmy Brucia's bar on Alvarado Street. Johnny was Spanish. He and his mother, Maria, entertained at local events doing flamenco demonstrations. He may also have been a singer. Steinbeck patronized Brucia's bar and quickly became friends with Garcia. Steinbeck wrote about his touching reunion with Johnny Garcia in *Travels with Charley.*

1937. Johnny Garcia, left, and Jimmy Brucia are inside Jimmy's tavern. It was located at 242 Alvarado Street, where a Doubletree hotel is located at this writing.
MONTEREY PUBLIC LIBRARY, CALIFORNIA HISTORY ROOM ARCHIVES

SPARKY AND TINY

*Sparky Enea and Tiny Colletti had made up a quarrel and were helping
Jimmy to celebrate his birthday.* —CHAPTER ELEVEN

Minor characters, though they were, Sparky Enea and Tiny Colleti were residents of Monterey. Both men were acquainted with Steinbeck in the 1930s, and they went with him as crewmen on the Western Flyer during the voyage to the Sea of Cortez in 1940. No one is certain how the trio originally met, but it is likely that Steinbeck was introduced to them at the harbor since he enjoyed fishing.

THE GROSS FAMILY

The whole Gross family came down with [influenza]. —CHAPTER SIXTEEN

The Gross family was prominent in Monterey during the 1930s. According to various *Polk* directories, E.B. Gross owned the E.B. Gross Cannery on the eastern end of Ocean View Avenue from the early 1920s to 1943, and his family lived at 178 Central Avenue in Pacific Grove. On June 18, 1943, Gross sold his cannery, but stated that he would remain active in his banking and real-estate ventures in Monterey, which he did.

EXCELENTÍSIMA MARIA ANTONIA FIELD

Excelentísima Maria Antonia Field had [influenza]. —CHAPTER SIXTEEN

Maria Antonia Field was born at her family home on December 5, 1885 and died on July 23, 1961. She was the great-granddaughter of Esteban Munras, who had been sent to Monterey by the King of Spain around 1820. Her mother was Catalina Munras and her father was Joseph Field. The King of Spain honored Maria for her charitable work by giving her the title Excelentísima. The original Munras home has since been incorporated within the Casa Munras Hotel at Munras and Fremont Streets.

1930s—Excelentísima Maria Antonia Field.

MONTEREY PUBLIC LIBRARY, CALIFORNIA HISTORY ROOM ARCHIVES

THE SPRAGUE FAMILY

"The Sprague kid had seen them and he says they ain't no bigger than this and they got little hands and feet and eyes." —CHAPTER SIXTEEN

During a fight between Joey and Willard in *Cannery Row*, the boys argue about "the Sprague kid," who claims to have seen fetuses in Doc's lab. In real life, the Sprague family lived in Pacific Grove. "Pop Sprague had glass-bottomed boats and boat rentals at Lovers Point in the summertime," Jimmy Willoughby explained in 1997. Locals Joe and Doris Bragdon recalled that "the Sprague family lived across from Doris' family on 18th Street in Pacific Grove. The family ran the boat concession at Lovers Point in Pacific Grove. Their son died as the result of an accident while he was in high school."

1940s. The Scotch Bakery sign
is visible in the lower half of
the photo.

PAT HATHAWAY PHOTO COLLECTION

Cannery Row is the gathered and scattered, tin and iron and rust and splintered wood, chipped pavement and weedy lots and junk heaps, sardine canneries of corrugated iron, honky tonks, restaurants and whore houses, and little crowded groceries, and laboratories and flophouses. —CANNERY ROW

CHAPTER 6

SURROUNDINGS

MOST OF THE LOCATIONS FROM *CANNERY ROW* ARE BASED ON real places in Monterey. Steinbeck included them with very few changes, strengthening the connection between his novel and the real town that inspired it. By using real places, Steinbeck paints a strikingly accurate portrait of local lives. Steinbeck's careful nuances draw the reader to the specifics of Monterey; his mention of the *new* post-office establishes the building as one built during his tenure in town. Many of the locations survived redevelopment projects, and Steinbeck enthusiasts can visit them.

Establishments

LA IDA

On such a morning and in such a light two soldiers and two girls strolled easily along the street. They had come out of La Ida and they were very tired and happy. —CHAPTER FOURTEEN

La Ida was a real brothel located at 851 Ocean View Avenue next to the Wing Chong Co., in exactly the location Steinbeck established it in the book. The restaurant was a front for the brothel in real life as well as in the novel.

La Ida, which locals often called "Edith's," opened in the early- to mid-1930s. Edith Luciani, who came from San Francisco to run the place,[52] was a large woman, weighing well over three hundred pounds, and was an outspoken person by nature. In the late 1930s, Joe Bragdon, a young cannery worker, recalled her yelling at him and his friends when they were on their way

1939. The La Ida Cafe and brothel is just to the right of the Wing Chong Co., which is directly behind the smokestack. The neon sign mentioned in the book is faintly visible on the building's front.

PAT HATHAWAY PHOTO COLLECTION

to work: "How would one of you guys like three hundred pounds of hot mama?" Edith's boyfriend (or perhaps he was her husband) was named Jimmy. Although Jimmy worked with Edith, their official relationship status remains a mystery since her friends took very little interest in such particulars.

2005. The La Ida/Kalisa's as it appeared until 2007. The Wing Chong Co. building is on the left.

Edith used both floors of the building; the restaurant, bar and kitchen were on the first floor and the brothel was on the second. The brothel consisted of five small rooms and a bathroom. The *Polk Directory*, which listed all local businesses as well as their owners, residences, and occupants, did not list La Ida until its 1937, 1939 and 1941 editions.

La Ida closed in 1941 when California's attorney general closed all the brothels in the state. At this writing the building, which sits directly across the street from the Monterey Bay Aquarium, houses a restaurant. From 1958 until February 2007, a Monterey local named Kalisa Moore leased the property and operated it. Due to her years of dedicated effort to keep the Steinbeck legacy alive in Monterey, Kalisa has been rightfully named "The Queen of Cannery Row."

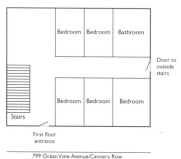

The Second Floor of La Ida

Bedroom | Bedroom | Bathroom

Door to outside stairs

Bedroom | Bedroom | Bedroom

Stairs

First floor entrance

799 Ocean View Avenue/Cannery Row

This illustration shows the layout of the upstairs of the La Ida brothel in the late 1930s. This illustration is based on a 1996 drawing by Jimmy Rodriquez.

2005. The upstairs at La Ida/Kalisa's was the brothel area in the 1930s.

JIMMY BRUCIA'S BAR

If Gay had not been a mechanic, he would not have fixed the car. If he had not
fixed it the owner wouldn't have taken him to Jimmy Brucia's
for a drink. —CHAPTER SEVENTEEN

Jimmy Brucia's bar was a popular Monterey establishment. Antonio Brucia, Jimmy's father and a leading member of the Italian community, established the bar at 242 Alvarado Street in 1927. When Antonio died in 1939, Jimmy had already been running the bar for several years. He continued to run the bar until his death in 1961, noted historian and journalist Bonnie Gartshore. Brucia's later became the Horseshoe Inn, but it was demolished in 1969 to make way for the Monterey Custom House Plaza.

RED'S FLYING A GAS STATION

Henri had taken up his post across the street at Red Williams' gas station . . .
[He] sat in a chair, leaned back against the lattice which concealed the door
of the men's toilet at Red Williams'. —CHAPTER SEVENTEEN

2005. This building occupies the site where Red Williams' Flying A station was once located.

Red Williams owned the Flying A service station on Lighthouse Avenue, just across from the real Holman's Department Store on Fountain Avenue. "The gas station did have lattice to cover the restroom doors, just as Steinbeck indicated. Instead of a chair, there was a stool for people to sit on," said Red's brother Florus. Bonnie Gartshore added, "Previous to opening the Flying A station in 1934, Red had a Shell station located on the corner of Lighthouse Avenue and David Street where the liquor store is now. Red's station was a favorite place for local people to come in, gather, and socialize.

Florus recalled, "John Steinbeck came in often since he and Red were good friends. Gabe would come in trying to get anything for free. He was always tinkering with cars, but not at the station." Florus also remembered that Red sold Steinbeck the small outboard motor that became known as the *Hansen Sea Cow* on the voyage to the Sea of Cortez. The station was the scene for other events, as well. Dottie Bicknell Sanchez stated, "I remember that Dad had gotten a set of new false teeth and he took them to Red's and either sold or traded them for a gallon of wine. My mother could have killed him."

HALF-WAY HOUSE BAR

One evening he [Doc] stopped in at the Halfway House because they had a draft beer he liked . . . —CHAPTER TWENTY-SEVEN

The Half-Way House was a real bar, but note that its name was hyphenated. Steinbeck eschewed the hyphen. The bar was located at 598 Lighthouse Avenue in New Monterey, a local designation for the area between the Presidio and David Avenue. It was the last bar before the town of Pacific Grove, which was a dry town at the time. In the 1930s, the Half-Way House was a beer bar owned by Jim Armstrong, facts that Jimmy Rodriquez and Charlie Nonella corraborate. Florus Williams recalled, "The last time I saw John Steinbeck was about 1947 and he was in the Half-Way House sitting alone, drinking, and watching people. I also saw Gabe Bicknell in there." Lifelong Monterey resident Bill Hyler

Early 1940s. The Half-Way House bar was located at 598 Lighthouse Avenue, on the northeast corner of Lighthouse Avenue and Hoffman Street.
MONTEREY PUBLIC LIBRARY,
CALIFORNIA HISTORY ROOM ARCHIVES

also recalled seeing John Steinbeck in the Half-Way House in the late 1930s.

When Hyler was asked what he was doing in the bar, since he was under-age at the time, he replied, "I was getting a hamburger. The place was famous for its hamburgers with special Half-Way House Salsa on them." Bill explained that the bar's original owner, Jim Armstrong, had the recipe for a

2005. This building occupies the former location of the Half-Way House bar.

superb salsa that made the hamburgers exceptionally good. Even though the bar was sold several times prior to being torn down, the recipe was never revealed. Olive Hyler, Bill's wife, received the recipe from Don Noggle, a past owner of the Half-Way House and her lifelong friend. For two decades the area's residents, including Steinbeck, frequented the Half-Way House and enjoyed drinks and its famous hamburger salsa.

The recipe for Half-Way House Salsa is provided by Bill Hyler for any reader who may want to recreate some authentic 1930s Monterey cuisine.

Half-Way House Salsa

10 large onions, finely chopped	1 1/2 cups wine vinegar
3 large cans of tomatoes, drained and diced	1 cup of peanut oil
	1 teaspoon of pepper
2 whole green chilies, diced	1/4 teaspoon of cumin powder
5 kosher dill pickles, diced	1/4 teaspoon of salt
3 large bell peppers, diced	chili pepper to taste

Combine all of the ingredients in a very large bowl. Mix and refrigerate overnight.

1930s. This aerial view of the Hotel del Monte shows its size and extravagance.

PAT HATHAWAY PHOTO COLLECTION

HOTEL DEL MONTE

But Josh Billings dies out at the Hotel del Monte. —CHAPTER ONE

The Hotel del Monte, where Josh Billings was supposed to have died, first opened in 1880 on Del Monte Avenue, across from the beach where the Naval Postgraduate School is currently located. A very large and luxurious hotel that catered to wealthy tourists, the Del Monte was destroyed by fire in 1887 and then rebuilt. Several wings of the old hotel are still used by the naval school. In 2005, local historian and Steinbeck enthusiast Neal Hotelling received a national award for his successful efforts to preserve the original portions of the Hotel del Monte that are on the grounds of the Naval Postgraduate School.

THE CHICKEN WALK

[The Palace Flophouse was . . .] past the cypress tree, across the railroad tracks, up a chicken walk with cleats. —CHAPTER ONE

1945. Locals used the chicken walk to get from Ocean View Avenue to Wave Street.

PETER STACKPOLE, MARTHA HEASLEY COX CENTER FOR STEINBECK STUDIES, SAN JOSE STATE UNIVERSITY

A chicken walk stood in the exact location John Steinbeck referred to in the book. It was little more than a wooden walkway that led from the railroad tracks up a small hill to the Palace. The term "chicken walk" originated on farms with raised chicken coops; the chickens entered their coops by means of a long, sloping board with ridges for traction. The walkway at the railroad had wooden strips across it to provide traction, reminding locals of a "chicken walk."

2005. The chicken walk came to be known as Bruce Ariss Way.

THE FROG POND

Frogs blink from its banks and deep ferns grow beside it. Deer and foxes come to drink from it, secretly in the morning and evening, and now and then a mountain lion crouched flat laps its water . . . It's everything a river should be. —CHAPTER THIRTEEN

There were a number of possible locations on the Carmel River that could have been the frog pond as described in the book. In the late 1930s and into the 1940s, there were places on the river that contained good pools for frogs and had orchards nearby—just as depicted in the book. That area of the river is located off Carmel Valley Road between Schulte and Berwick Roads.[53] Since the time of the book's setting, the riverbed has changed a great deal, due to the torrents of water caused by winter rains.

HARTNELL GULCH

Where the new post office is there used to be a deep gulch with water flowing in it and a little footbridge over it. On one side of the gulch was a fine old adobe and on the other the doctor who handled all the sickness, birth, and death in the town. —CHAPTER TWELVE

In the novel, a young boy and a small dog find Josh Billings' intestines carelessly thrown into the Hartnell Gulch, causing a great uproar in the town and leading to a minor revolt against the doctor. The Hartnell Gulch extended from Soledad Drive to the Cooper-Molera Adobe. Many people have questioned which house served as the old adobe Steinbeck wrote about. Local legend favors the Stokes Adobe at 500 Hartnell Street since an earlier resident, Hattie Gragg, was a friend of Steinbeck. In the late 1800s, the community hospital

2005. The Hartnell Gulch, or what remains of it.

and several medical buildings that were located on Hartnell Street across from the post office, near the gulch where Steinbeck placed them in the book.[54] Through the years, parts of the gulch were covered over, then channeled into

2005. The Stokes Adobe, which is located at 500 Hartnell Street.

culverts, and built upon. In the 1980s, Hartnell Gulch Park was created by building a footpath along the portion of the gulch adjacent to the Monterey Public Library at 625 Pacific Street.

SEA PRIDE PACKING COMPANY

The Hediondo Cannery is hiring guys. —CHAPTER SEVEN

There was a cannery located next to Ed Ricketts' lab. Steinbeck named its *Cannery Row* counterpart Hediondo, which means "stinking" in Spanish, aptly descriptive for the fishing and canning season on Cannery Row. Bonnie Gartshore noted that in the 1930s, two canneries flanked the Pacific Biological Lab: Sea Pride Packing Company was on the west side and the Del Mar Canning Company was on the east. There was no cannery named Hediondo in Monterey, but from the description of the location of the Hediondo Cannery, it appears to be patterned after Sea Pride Packing. Period photos show that the Del Mar Cannery practically shared a wall with the lab. However, on the Sea Pride side, there was a tree and plenty of room for the old Chinaman to disappear. The Monterey Bay Aquarium and a retail store occupy the space formerly taken by the Sea Pride Packing Company.

HERMANN'S

In Monterey before he even started, he felt hungry and stopped at Hermann's
for a hamburger and beer. —CHAPTER SEVENTEEN

Hermann's Coffee Shop was located in the Osio Adobe at 380 Alvarado Street, wrote Bonnie Gartshore. It was a popular restaurant in Monterey; in the novel Doc stops at Hermann's Café for a hamburger and beer before departing on a collecting expedition. The adobe was built in 1848. Harold J. McLean was the restaurant manager and became the owner in 1930. Because McLean was such an affable host, Hermann's became a successful restaurant where Steinbeck occasionally stopped to eat. McLean sold the restaurant in 1959. At this writing, the name Hermann's can be seen written in tile lettering on the ground level at the front door of the adobe. The building now houses the Monterey Convention Center and the Monterey Chamber of Commerce.

1949. Four patrons are shown standing on the tiles in front of the restaurant. Hermann's Coffee Shop was located in this building—which now houses the Monterey Chamber of Commerce.
MONTEREY PUBLIC LIBRARY, CALIFORNIA HISTORY ROOM ARCHIVES

Late 1920s. Hermann's restaurant, with its wooden beamed front, is in the old Rodriquez-Osio building. The structure to the left of Hermann's has survived.

PAT HATHAWAY PHOTO COLLECTION

1950 Hermann's Coffee Shop can be seen on the left as it appeared five years after
Cannery Row was published.

MONTEREY PUBLIC LIBRARY, CALIFORNIA HISTORY ROOM ARCHIVES

Reference Points

While the following spots are mere mentions in *Cannery Row*, they are local places that John Steinbeck included for authenticity. They are listed here in alphabetical order.

ADOBE BAR

The name for the Adobe Bar probably came from the various establishments on Alvarado Street that included "El Adobe" in their names. It was a popular name, as evidenced by the El Adobe Bar that was listed at 326 Alvarado Street from 1907 to 1917 in city directories. The 1926 *Polk Directory* for Monterey listed the El Adobe Building, which had been built in 1819, at 378 Alvarado Street, the El Adobe Hospital at 602 Abrego, and the El Adobe tamale parlor on Fremont Street.

1920s. The El Adobe is shown on the left of the El Adobe Building.
PAT HATHAWAY PHOTO COLLECTION

ALVARADO STREET

Alvarado Street was built in the 1800s, and is still the main street of downtown Monterey. Many important locations from *Cannery Row* stood on this street, and can be found on the map on page 25.

Late 1920s. This view looks down Alvarado Street toward the harbor. The store with the "candy" sign was The Poppy.

PAT HATHAWAY PHOTO COLLECTION

CARMEL VALLEY ROAD

Carmel Valley Road has existed since the mid-1930s. The valley was sparsely populated in the 1930s, but the population has expanded greatly and the Carmel Valley Road is heavily used. The road runs southeast from Highway 1 through the valley, Carmel Valley Village, and ends at Miller's Ranch, a few miles west of the town of Greenfield.

EL CARMELO CEMETERY

There was and still is a scenic cemetery located at 65 Asilomar Boulevard in Pacific Grove near the Point Piños Lighthouse. The "pretty little cemetery" Steinbeck referred to is named the El Carmelo Cemetery and was built in 1889. Since 1948 it has been operated by the City of Pacific Grove.

1933. The gates of the "pretty little cemetery."
MONTEREY PUBLIC LIBRARY,
CALIFORNIA HISTORY ROOM ARCHIVES

2005. The cemetery gates show the effects of time.

CHINA POINT

China Point is the small piece of land jutting into Monterey Bay just west of the Monterey Bay Aquarium. It was named after the Chinese immigrants who built a village nearby in

pre-1906. The village of China Point as it appeared before the fire in 1906.
PAT HATHAWAY PHOTO COLLECTION

1932. This aerial view shows China Point. The buildings are part of Hopkins Marine Station.
PAT HATHAWAY PHOTO COLLECTION

1851. The village was destroyed by fire in 1906; now Hopkins Marine Station occupies China Point.

DEL MONTE BEACH

Del Monte Beach is located east of the Monterey harbor along Del Monte Avenue, across from the Hotel del Monte. Occasionally, severe storms forced fishing boats ashore there. The Naval Postgraduate School now occupies the hotel area.

THE GOLDEN STAIRS

Flora Woods had a second brothel, the Golden Stairs, located at the corner of Franklin and Figueroa streets. It was in a large two-story building located across from a softball field. According to Jimmy Rodriquez, "It was called the Golden Stairs because the customers had to go up a set of stairs located on the outside of the building to get to the entertainment." Like the other brothels in town, it was listed as a restaurant. Sal Genovese, a local fisherman, said that the Golden Stairs was not as nice as Flora's, "as it did not have a large parlor, jukebox or the other amenities available at Flora's."

2005. This building at the corner of Franklin and Figueroa Streets marks the former location of the Golden Stairs, which was Flora's brothel "by the baseball field."

1970s. The Golden Stairs, which was Flora's brothel by the baseball field, was located on the second floor of this building.

MICHAEL K. HEMP

GRIMES POINT

1930s. Grimes Point is approximately twenty-seven miles south of Carmel.

PAT HATHAWAY PHOTO COLLECTION

Grimes Point juts into the Pacific Ocean between Pfeiffer and Partington Ridges, about thirty miles south of Monterey. Grimes Point was named for Edward A. Grimes, an Englishman who came to California in 1875. He worked for his uncle, James Meadows, in Carmel Valley. In 1879, he married Ellen Post of Big Sur, and homesteaded property four miles south of the Post Ranch—which is now on Highway 1.

HATTON FIELDS

The area called Hatton Fields is located to the west of Hatton Canyon between Highway 1 and the southern limits of Carmel, where Steinbeck placed it in the book. It was originally part of the *Rancho Cañada de La Segundo.* According to Bonnie Gartshore, the Hatton family purchased it and established a dairy on the land. It was later developed as a residential area.

HOPKINS MARINE STATION

The Hopkins Marine Station is located near the ocean just west of the Monterey Boat Works and Hovden's Cannery. In 1892, Hopkins Marine Station was established at Lovers Point in Pacific Grove. In 1916 it relocated to China Point and opened the next year as Stanford University Hopkins Marine Station.[55] The station is a marine biology research center. According to Jackson J. Benson, Steinbeck's biographer, Steinbeck and his sister attended a summer session at the marine station, taking three classes in 1923.

1940s. This photo of Hopkins Marine Station was taken from nearby Lovers Point.

JACKS PEAK ROAD

The real Jacks Peak Road, named for David Jacks, is located in a residential area and runs through a county park. Jacks came to Monterey in 1850 and eventually owned a vast amount of real estate. Steinbeck inserted an apostrophe and called it Jack's Peak Road.

JAMESBURG

A very small group of homes in a village called Jamesburg still stands in Carmel Valley. Jamesburg is located 2.2 miles off County Road G-12, on Tassajara Road.

2005. Jamesburg in Carmel Valley.

1931. The Point Piños Lighthouse.

MONTEREY PUBLIC LIBRARY, CALIFORNIA HISTORY ROOM ARCHIVES

THE POINT PIÑOS LIGHTHOUSE

The formal name of the lighthouse is the Point Piños Lighthouse. It was built in 1854 and is the oldest continuously operating lighthouse on the California coast.

2005. The Point Piños Lighthouse remains in operation.

LIGHTHOUSE AVENUE

Lighthouse Avenue remains the main commercial street connection between Monterey and Pacific Grove. Businesses on Lighthouse Avenue that were mentioned in *Cannery Row* include the Half-Way House, Red Williams' gas station, Holman's Department Store and the Scotch Bakery, now Favaloro's Big Night Bistro.

1932. Lighthouse Avenue in Pacific Grove as it appeared at the time of the book's setting.
PAT HATHAWAY PHOTO COLLECTION

MONTEREY BOAT WORKS

The Monterey Bay Boat Works is located a short distance west of where the Monterey Bay Aquarium now stands, the spot where Steinbeck placed it in the novel. In the 1920s, a man named Smith owned the boat works. In the early 1930s, Angelo Siino, a boat builder

2005. The Monterey Boat Works used this building from the 1920s until it closed in the 1950s. It became an instructional facility for the Hopkins Marine Station.

from Italy, bought it and named it the Monterey Boat Works. The Siino family built many of the boats used by local fishermen and commercial abalone divers. Many of the canneries' floating fish hoppers were built there as well.

HOVDEN CANNERY

The place Steinbeck called Morden Cannery was actually called the Hovden Cannery. Based on the route the boys took across the railroad tracks and down to Cannery Row, the first cannery they could have thrown rocks at was Hovden's Cannery.

PETERS GATE

There are two sets of Peters Gates. One is on Alameda and Munras Streets, and the other is on the corner of Grove and Alameda Streets. Willis Polk designed the gates in the late 1890s for the Bohemian Club of San Francisco, which was interested in the land tract. The gates were named for Charles Rollo Peters who lived on the tract. The gate on Munras Street has been maintained over the years and the name Peters Gate is clearly visible. Though Steinbeck referred to them as Peter's Gate, signs on the gates themselves omit the apostrophe.

Early 1940s. These ladies are landscaping the area adjacent to one set of Peters Gates. "Peters Gate" is written near the top of the column.

MONTEREY PUBLIC LIBRARY, CALIFORNIA HISTORY ROOM ARCHIVES

2006. One of the two existing sets of Peters Gates.

POINT LOBOS

Point Lobos is a picturesque headland that marks the south end of Carmel Bay. The beauty of the area has long been an attraction for writers and artists and has seen many different uses. Point Lobos has been a pasture for cattle, the site of a whaling station, an abalone cannery, and a coal-shipping location. It has also served as a shooting location for a number of films. Point Lobos is part of the Point Lobos State Reserve, and is one of California's most scenic public parks.

POINT SUR

Point Sur juts out into the Pacific Ocean about twenty-five miles south of Carmel.

1930s. The Point Sur Lighthouse as it appeared at the time *Cannery* Row was set.

PAT HATHAWAY PHOTO COLLECTION

1946. The Poppy on Alvarado Street was five doors away from the movie theater Steinbeck mentioned.

MONTEREY PUBLIC LIBRARY, CALIFORNIA HISTORY ROOM ARCHIVES

THE POPPY

The Poppy café and confectionery was located at 434 Alvarado Street and a movie theater was a short distance away. Steinbeck probably changed the name from The Poppy to the Golden Poppy in honor of California's state flower.

2005. This building occupies the former site of The Poppy.

NEW POST OFFICE

Monterey's new post office opened in 1933, at 565 Hartnell Street. The post office still serves as the main U.S. Postal Service office in Monterey; the original Monterey post office was the first post office in California.

1938. The "new post office" is still in use at this writing.
MONTEREY PUBLIC LIBRARY, CALIFORNIA HISTORY ROOM ARCHIVES

SAN CARLOS HOTEL

The San Carlos Hotel was a very large, well-appointed hotel located at the corner of Franklin and Main Streets.

1930s. The San Carlos Hotel in downtown Monterey.
PAT HATHAWAY PHOTO COLLECTION

SCOTCH BAKERY

The Scotch Bakery was been in the same location, 545 Lighthouse Avenue, since at least the 1930s. In 2006 the business became Favaloro's Big Night Bistro.

2005. The Scotch Bakery.

THE THRIFT MARKET

There was a Thrift Market in the 1930s in New Monterey. During the Depression, Thrift Markets sold inexpensive goods to local patrons. In the 1937 *Polk Directory*, Monterey Market was listed at 606-614 Lighthouse Avenue in New Monterey. In 2008, the Bamboo Reef Dive Store occupied the building.

2001. In the 1930s, this building housed the Thrift Market.

GREAT TIDE POOL

The Great Tide Pool is located in the tidal area just south of Point Piños. Although there are many tide pools along the shoreline of Ocean View Boulevard in Pacific Grove, Ed Ricketts, Jr., told historian Pat Hathaway that his father did not use those areas due to the pollution in the water from the canneries.

TOM WORK'S LAND

T.A. Work, a native of the Shetland Islands, and a prominent Monterey County banker, rancher and financier, came to the Monterey Peninsula in 1885. Tom Work's yard stood on David Avenue, from Lighthouse Avenue to the current location of the Monterey Bay Aquarium. Among his other land-holdings were two thousand acres "across the head of the bay," which later became part of Fort Ord.

2005. "Tom Work's land" is shown across Monterey Bay.

PART THREE

EVENTS AND HAPPENINGS

The knowledge of the party for Doc was no sudden thing. It did not burst out full blown. People knew about it but let it grow gradually like a pupa in the cocoons of their imaginations.

—CHAPTER TWENTY-FIVE

1930s. This unpaved road, leading to the Carmel Valley River, is the type that Mack and the boys would have taken on their great frog-hunt adventure.

Over a period of years Doc dug himself into Cannery Row to an extent not even he suspected. He became the fountain of philosophy and science and art.
—CHAPTER FIVE

CHAPTER 7

LIFE WITH ED

COLLECTING SPECIMENS

Hysterically the frogs displaced from their placid spots swam ahead of the crazy thrashing feet and the feet came on. A few frogs lost their heads . . . but the majority decided to leave this pool forever, to find a new home in a new country where this kind of thing didn't happen . . . A wave of frantic, frustrated frogs, big ones, little ones, brown ones, green ones, men frogs and women frogs, a wave of them broke over the bank . . . Two men gathered them like berries. —CHAPTER FIFTEEN

Ed Ricketts frequently employed some of the bums as collectors of the various specimens he needed for his business since he required a constant supply of many types of tide pool creatures. Ed often took a collector with him or sent him alone with specific instructions for what specimens he required. Even though the descriptive term "bums" is used, and despite their sometimes-wayward ways, those men had to be knowledgeable and capable collectors to be employed by Ed Ricketts. Charlie Nonella, Gabe Bicknell, Louie Nonella and Chet Bushnell all worked for Ricketts at one time or another.[56]

The following letter that Gabe Bicknell wrote to a Mr. Dahl on March 5, 1949, demonstrates just how capable the bums could be as collectors.

> I have hesitated to write you in any detail about the collecting you spoke of until I saw John Steinbeck. I saw John today and he assures me that the "P.B.L." [Pacific Biological Lab] won't operate again ever.
>
> Now if you are still interested in my services as a collector, I will be glad to try and get you whatever specimens you need.
>
> We have tides coming around the middle of March. I have gone as far south as Long Beach for 'Doc,' and have had considerable experience on inner-tide [sic] specimens.[57]

"Same price for frogs?" Mack asked. "Five cents apiece?" —CHAPTER NINE

Ed paid his collectors, both adults and children, five cents apiece for frogs. According to Dottie Bicknell Sanchez, he also bought butterflies and cats. The Carmel River contained a great deal of good frog habitat along its course through the Carmel Valley to the ocean just south of Carmel. In a letter sent to a friend in 1937, Ed stated, "Terribly rushed, the boys are sending in frog shipments almost daily, over seven hundred yesterday. And cats and crayfish still coming in, but not more than enough for orders."[58]

As a youngster in the early 1930s, George Fraley, a lifelong area resident, recalled catching and then selling cats to Ed for twenty-five cents each. He, like the other young entrepreneurs of Cannery Row, would take their quarters to the Wing Chong Co. to buy candy.

Cat Skeletons

It was well known in Monterey that Ed Ricketts bought cats (from local people, mainly kids) which he embalmed and then sold to school biology departments. What is not widely known is that in addition to the market for embalmed cats, Ed had another feline market—cat skeletons. Because getting a skeleton from a cat was a very messy and time-consuming job, Ed showed Bill Hyler how to obtain a skeleton with little effort. At that time, the late 1930s, Bill was a teenaged cannery worker who worked part time, helping Ed to gather specimens at Point Piños.

Bill was told to get an empty five-gallon tomato paste can from a cannery. Ed then had him remove the top of the can and tie a string across the top. The cat's body was placed in the can, which was then lowered into the ocean on a rope. Bill remembered that the best place to do this—and not get caught—was under the Critchlow Engine Repair shop on the old Fisherman's Wharf. After about two weeks in the ocean, only the skeleton remained. Bill recalled that Ed paid him twenty-five cents an hour.

ED'S SAFE

Once the safe got locked by mistake and no one knew the combination. And in the safe was an open can of sardines and a piece of Roquefort cheese. —CHAPTER FIVE

At one point Ed's safe contained a piece of cheese, but the safe was not locked. The incident occurred in 1936. On November 25, 1936, a fire had started in the cannery building next to the lab, destroying the lab and other buildings on the ocean side of Ocean View Avenue. According to Ed Ricketts, Jr., neither the door to Ed's lab nor the door to his safe were locked. Bruce Ariss, who was a friend of Steinbeck and Ricketts, was with Ed the morning after the fire and recalled, "We found Ed forlornly inspecting the flattened rubble that had once been the lab. Everything was gone—his library, his vast collection of scientific papers, his fine record collection, all the stored bottles of specimens and, of course, all my beautiful jars of colors. The only thing that survived was a fireproof safe that had stood beside the rolltop desk in the upstairs office. It was sitting in the ashes on the ground. Ed opened it, and found some smelly cheese he had stored there the day before the fire."[59]

ED'S MUSIC

A great phonograph stands against the wall with hundreds of records
lined up behind it. —CHAPTER FIVE

Ed Ricketts had a wonderful phonograph. Ricketts' friend Pol Verbeck, an accomplished electrician from Belgium, built the phonograph for him. Verbeck built one for Steinbeck as well.[60] In a 1938 letter to a friend, Ed said, "Also, most recent news, I have now a phonograph and radio receiver built by Pol Verbeck, who made Dick Albee's and John's fine sets."[61]

And the great shrouds of music came out of the lab at any time of
the day or night. —CHAPTER SEVENTEEN

Ed Ricketts truly enjoyed listening to fine music on his phonograph. Ricketts liked classical music and he especially liked the Gregorian chants, the masses of Palestrina and the work of Scarlatti and Monteverde. His favorite was Bach's "Art of the Fugue."[62] Ricketts occasionally played his music loud enough to be heard some distance away. "I have talked to others who heard Ed's phonograph music, but it must have been mainly at night," wrote Joe Bragdon, a teenage cannery worker who befriended Ed.

Before her death in 2002, Irene Longueira stated, "On several occasions, I would look out my window on the east side of my house and see Ed Ricketts and John Steinbeck sitting on a small patch of grass, drinking red wine and listening to classical music from his lab. Since I lived straight up from the lab on Wave Street, that music was very loud."

When the lights went on and the curtains were drawn, and the Gregorian music played
on the phonograph, Mack used to look down on the lab from the Palace Flophouse.
He knew Doc had a girl in there. —CHAPTER SEVENTEEN

Ed played his music for his own benefit, but also used it to help John Steinbeck through a difficult period. "Once, when I had suffered an overwhelming emotional upset, I went to the laboratory to stay with him [Ed]. I was dull and speechless with shock and pain. He used music on me like med-

1936. Bystanders on Ocean View Avenue watch as Ed's lab burns to the ground.
PAT HATHAWAY PHOTO COLLECTION

icine. Late in the night when he should have been asleep, he played music for me on his great phonograph—even when I was asleep he played it knowing that its soothing would get into my dark confusion."[63]

DOC'S BEER MILK SHAKES

Doc knew wearily that he couldn't explain, couldn't tell the truth. "I've got a bladder complaint," he said. "Bipalychaetorsonectomy, the doctors called it. I'm supposed to drink a beer milk shake. Doctor's orders." —CHAPTER SEVENTEEN

According to his son, Ed Ricketts did not drink beer milk shakes; in fact, he had an intense dislike for milk. However, Ed once drank milk and rum as a cure for an ulcer. A doctor suggested that Ricketts drink milk to help with

2005. These photos are representative of the many tide pools in the Point Piños area, where Ed Ricketts gathered specimens.

the ulcer's symptoms. After trying the milk, Ricketts found it so disagreeable that he asked the doctor for permission to add some rum. The doctor sensed he was fighting a losing battle, so he gave Ricketts his permission to add a few drops of rum to the milk. As John Steinbeck noted, the process fascinated Ed's friends because by the end of the month Ricketts was adding several drops of milk to the rum and his ulcer was cured.[64]

DOC WALKED THROUGH THE SOUTH

Once when Doc was at the University of Chicago he had love trouble and had worked too hard. He thought it would be nice to take a very long walk. He put on a little knapsack and walked through Indiana and Kentucky and North Carolina and Georgia clear to Florida . . . Because he loved true things, he tried to explain . . . —CHAPTER SEVENTEEN

Ed Ricketts walked as far south as Georgia, not Florida as depicted in the *Cannery Row*. In the early 1920s, Ed took a train to Indianapolis and, wearing

Doc was collecting marine animals in the Great Tide Pool on the tip of the Peninsula.
—CHAPTER SIX

a knapsack, walked through Indiana, Kentucky, North Carolina and Georgia. According to Steinbeck's biographer J.J. Benson, Ed undertook this incredible journey out of a simple desire to see the countryside.

ED AND THE DEAD GIRL

A girl's face looked up at him, a pretty, pale girl with dark hair . . . It seemed to Doc
that he had looked at it for many minutes, and the face burned into his picture memory . . .
Very slowly he raised his hand and let the brown weed float back
over her face. —CHAPTER EIGHTEEN

According to Jean Ariss, she and Ed Ricketts walked near Point Lobos State Reserve and found a dead girl in a tide pool.[65] Steinbeck merely changed the location for *Cannery Row.*

pre-1927. The early method of transferring sardines to the canneries was very inefficient and time-consuming.

Holman's set up a double bed in their window. When the skater broke the world's record he was going to come down and sleep right in the window without taking off his skates.
—CHAPTER NINETEEN

CHAPTER 8
LIFE ON THE ROW

THE WININ' JUG

Eddie poured glasses half or two-thirds full into the funnel. The resulting punch which he took back to the Palace was always interesting and sometimes surprising. —CHAPTER SEVEN

Eddie, the understudy bartender at La Ida, would pour unfinished drinks into a gallon jug called the "winin' jug" and bring the mixture home for the residents of the Palace Flophouse. The "winin' jug" was most likely tied to a story Steinbeck heard in the 1920s when he lived and worked in New York City. Steinbeck knew a speakeasy handyman named Ducky. Ducky received a jug filled with leftover drinks as part of his pay. The bartender would use a funnel to pour the unfinished drinks into a jug, and gave it to Ducky once it was full.[66] In addition to this, John Steinbeck told his son, Thom, that many bars in Monterey collected the unused drinks and sold the results to the bums. The concoction was called a "Blue Duck."

THE WATCHMAN'S SUICIDE

Before Alfy the present watchman took over, there was a tragedy at the Bear Flag Restaurant, which saddened everyone . . . Depressed and unhappy that he couldn't join the gang, William's hand rose and the ice pick snapped into his heart. —CHAPTER THREE

The suicide in the book was based on an actual death that occurred in Flora's home at 524 Van Buren Street on March 2, 1933. The man who killed himself, Henry Wojciechowski, used an ice pick to commit suicide, just as Steinbeck described. The man had lived at Flora's house as a boarder since at least 1930.[67]

PARTIES AT THE LAB

The nature of parties has been imperfectly studied. It is, however, generally understood that a party has a pathology, that it is a kind of an individual that is very likely to be a perverse individual. And it is also generally understood that a party hardly ever goes the way it is planned or intended. —CHAPTER THIRTY

A frog party in the lab, involving the many different levels of Cannery Row society, did not take place as it was described in the book.[68] The reality was that bums, collectors and other denizens of Cannery Row were not allowed upstairs in the lab. It was not that Ed Ricketts was against parties, but he valued his home, workplace and book collection too much to risk damaging it by having a party that was sure to get out of control. Ed Ricketts, John Steinbeck and their friends certainly had their share of parties; however, the attendees did not include the "regulars" of Cannery Row.

> *The lights blazed in the laboratory. The front door hung sideways by one hinge.*
> *The floor was littered with broken glass. Phonograph records, some broken,*
> *some only nicked, were strewn about . . . And it was empty,*
> *it was over.* —CHAPTER TWENTY

Ed had already had one disastrous experience in the early 1930s with Gabe and his friends that resulted in a great deal of damage to the basement part of his lab. On this occasion, while Ed was away on a frog-collecting trip, Gabe and the boys went into the lower portion of the lab and, after drinking the alcohol kept there, the boys caused considerable damage to the specimen jars and other equipment.[69] After such a stunt, the boys were never again allowed upstairs in the lab.

Steinbeck took several events, such as that one, combined them with his gifted ability as a storyteller, and created a party that he would most likely have wanted to attend. He even had a fictional Mr. and Mrs. "Gay" attend the party, a clear tribute to Gabe Bicknell. Again drawing on fact to color his story, Steinbeck accurately portrayed Ricketts' behavior. Just like in the book, many real-life gatherings at the lab ended with Ricketts reading "Black Marigolds" aloud.[70] According to Steinbeck, "Black Marigolds," an eleventh-century Sanskrit poem, was a favorite love poem of Ed Ricketts.[71]

CANNERY DIVING

> *I wonder whatever happened to that guy McKinley Moran.*
> *Remember that deep sea diver?* —CHAPTER THIRTEEN

Diving, by its nature is difficult and dangerous; however, the equipment divers used only increased the dangers. The divers wore a cumbersome deep-sea suit and helmet that, with the required amount of lead weights, totaled about 150 pounds. They usually performed their tasks in water with very low visibility and were subject to constant wave action. It is indeed a remarkable testimony to the divers of Cannery Row that so few of them were able to accomplish such a large job—one that was so vital to Cannery Row's ultimate expansion and subsequent fame. Without their brave efforts, Cannery Row would never have become, "a poem, a stink, grating noise, a quality of light, a tone, a habit, a nostalgia, a dream."

1930s. Andy Skov helps well-known Cannery Row diver Eddie Bushnell get dressed in his gear prior to diving on a pipeline.

FROM *UNDERSEAS LOG* (EDDIE BUSHNELL, 1947)

Divers were needed to help the boats unload their catches. Without the protection of a breakwater, it was impractical to build piers out from the canneries, since the weather would surely destroy them. This was only a minor inconvenience in the beginning, but by the mid-1920s fishing boats with much larger capacities were coming into use.

The new fishing boats employed the mechanically operated purse seine, which enabled far larger sardine catches; however, because the canneries had no piers, the new boats could not unload at the most convenient spot.

Consequently, the canneries had to develop a more efficient process for unloading the larger catches. To that end, Knut Hovden, owner of the

1940s. Fishing boats unloaded their catches into two wooden hoppers. The sardines then moved through an underwater pipeline to the canneries.

PAT HATHAWAY PHOTO COLLECTION

1938. The barrels supporting a pipeline are about to be sunk, dropping the pipeline into place.

GEORGE FRALEY COLLECTION

Hovden Cannery, invented the wooden hopper. The hopper was moored about two hundred yards offshore and the boats unloaded their catch into it. The sardines were drawn from the hopper to the canneries by means of water flowing through an underwater pipeline. Using this method, the canneries could handle all the sardines the fishermen could catch. In fact, the pipelines became the arteries through which the lifeblood of Cannery Row flowed. Steinbeck referred to the visible pipeline tails, extending from the ocean floor to the canneries, when he wrote, "The deep-laden boats pull in against the coast where the canneries dip their tails into the bay." The diver's job was to install and maintain the vital pipelines that carried the sardines from the hoppers to the canneries.

The concept was rather simple: the boats unloaded their catch into the hoppers and the sardines flowed through the pipelines to the canneries. However, the reality of the operation was anything but simple. To install the pipelines and connect them to the hoppers required laying six

1938. Diver Eddie Bushnell is waiting for his helmet to be secured.

GEORGE FRALEY COLLECTION

hundred to seven hundred feet of steel pipeline on a rocky bottom, then connecting it to the bottom of the hopper with a large-diameter rubber hose. From 1927 to 1938, the divers constructed the pipeline by connecting individual twelve-foot sections of pipe and bolting them together on the bottom. From 1938 on, the pipeline was a single piece made of welded sections, which was then floated to the proper place and sunk.

1946. George Fraley, the nephew of Eddie Bushnell, is ready to dive on a pipeline.

GEORGE FRALEY COLLECTION

A pipeline could become inoperable for a number of reasons, such as being clogged with sardines, having a twisted or broken rubber hose, or having a hole caused by corrosion. When a pipeline wasn't working properly, all or part of the cannery had to be shut down and divers were called to repair the problem. In the meantime, hundreds of workers were sent home without pay until the problem was repaired.

THE REVERSE ASCENT OF CARMEL HILL

He stopped, let the truck back around and aimed it down the hill. Then he gave it the gas and the reverse pedal. And the reverse was not worn. The truck crawled steadily and slowly but backward up Carmel Hill. —CHAPTER ELEVEN

Cannery Row resident Charlie Nonella commented "in the mid-1930s, the Carmel Hill Road was much steeper than it is now. Model Ts routinely backed up the hill. It was not unusual to see four or five cars backing up the hill at one time."[72] There are a couple of reasons why early Model Ts had to back up the hill. First, they had no fuel pump. The gas tank was located under the driver's seat and when near empty, the only way the engine could get fuel on a steep hill was to back up so that the gas in the tank was higher than the carburetor. Steinbeck describes another equally valid reason: the low-gear clutch bands would often wear thin, but since the reverse gear was not used as often, its bands were often in better shape and could take the hill without slipping.

1932. The flagpole skater performs a dangerous trick.

PAT HATHAWAY PHOTO COLLECTION

THE FLAGPOLE SKATER

. . . for Holman's Department Store had employed not a flagpole sitter but a flagpole skater. On a tall mast on top of the store he had a little round platform and there he was on skates going around and around . . . He was out to set a new record for being on skates on a platform. —CHAPTER SEVENTEEN

A roller skater performed on a platform on top of the flagpole over Holman's Department Store beginning on June 19, 1932. He skated continuously for fifty-one hours. Steinbeck created an imaginative solution to the skater's periodic needs. He imagined that the skater used a can to relieve himself, but according to Florus Williams the skater actually came down from the flagpole.

June 19, 1932. This view shows Holman's Department Store on Lighthouse Avenue in Pacific Grove with the flagpole skater on his platform atop the building.

PAT HATHAWAY PHOTO COLLECTION

ANDY FROM SALINAS
AND THE "OLD CHINAMAN"

. . . the loneliness—the desolate cold aloneness of the landscape made Andy whimper . . .
Andy was the only boy who ever did that and
he never did it again. —CHAPTER FOUR

These events were based on real events from Steinbeck's childhood. Herb Heinricks, who lived in Salinas, told Joe Bragdon that he had been a good friend of Steinbeck in grade school. One afternoon in Salinas, Steinbeck dared Herb to chant "Ching Chong Chinaman sitting on a rail, along came a white man who cut off his tail" to a passing Chinese man. The Chinese man heard the taunt, caught Herb, and gave him a thrashing.

Minor Happenings

FLORA'S IRS WOES

Dora was having trouble with her income tax, for she was entangled in that
curious enigma which said the business was illegal and
then taxed her for it. —CHAPTER SIXTEEN

1936. The *Monterey Trader's* front-page article regarding Flora Woods' income tax problems. Note her name is misspelled.

MONTEREY PUBLIC LIBRARY, CALIFORNIA HISTORY ROOM ARCHIVES

Flora Woods definitely had troubles with the Internal Revenue Service. As reported in the *Monterey Trader* on April 3, 1936, IRS officials were investigating the fact that she had never filed an income tax return. Despite the personal trouble it must have caused her, Flora's IRS woes had very little effect on her business.

FOURTH OF JULY PARADE

Well—in about half an hour the Fourth of July parade is going to pass on Lighthouse
Avenue. By just turning their heads, they [Mack and the boys] can see it, by
standing up they can watch it . . . Now I'll bet you a quart of beer they
won't even turn their heads —CHAPTER TWENTY-THREE

"There were parades on Lighthouse Avenue to celebrate the Fourth of July," according to Florus Williams. They were very popular with Monterey locals. Steinbeck probably attended them when he lived there.

CHARACTERS, SOURCES AND NOTES

FICTIONAL CHARACTERS

The following are people and places for whom, despite thorough research, no real corollary could be found in Monterey. They may have been figments of Steinbeck's imagination, created solely for use in the novel.

Horace Abbeville	Mr. Carriaga	Doctor Merrivale
The Greek cook at Flora's	Mr. Ryan	The three Willoughby girls
Dr. W.T. Waters	The Captain	Richard Frost
A man named Rattle	The Ransel Kids	Mary and Tom Talbot
Francis Almones	Blaisdell, the Poet	Joey and Willard

SOURCES

In the course of researching this book, the author had the pleasure of coming into contact with many of the people whose lives intersected both Steinbeck's *Cannery Row* and Steinbeck's life on the real Cannery Row. Only formal interviews are noted here; all the denizens of Cannery Row are thanked for their assistance and insights over the years.

JOE BRAGDON, avid Steinbeck enthusiast and historian, worked in the Monterey canneries in the late 1930s. Interviewed October 22, 2004; correspondence May 26, 1997, May 27, 1997, June 2, 1999.

DENNIS COPELAND is the archivist for the California Room at the Monterey Public Library. Correspondence March 28, 2005, March 21, 2006.

GEORGE FRALEY is a lifelong Monterey area resident. Interviewed November 10, 2006.

BONNIE GARTSHORE was for many years a reporter for the *Monterey Peninsula Herald* and a Monterey historian and author. Correspondence May 14, 1996, February 27, 2000.

SAL GENOVESE was a fisherman in Monterey from 1934 to 1964. Interviewed September 18, 1998.

PAT HATHAWAY is one of California's premier photo archivists. Interviewed March 3, 2006.

HENRY COUNTY, INDIANA, HISTORICAL SOCIETY, INC. Correspondence August 17, 1995.

NEAL AND BETTINA HOTELLING are avid and knowledgeable Steinbeck enthusiasts. Interviewed December 9, 2004; correspondence March 20, 2005.

BILL HYLER was a cannery worker and helper for Ed Ricketts ("Doc"). Interviewed March 26, 2006; correspondence April 24, 2006.

BILL JOHNK is the master craftsman who built the incredible scale models of Cannery Row buildings. Interviewed March 7, 2006.

IRENE LONGUEIRA lived in the same house at 800 Wave Street from 1928 until her death in 2002. Interviewed October 22, 1995, January 16, 1996, January 21, 1996, October 25, 1999.

A. ROYAL MANAKA is the son of Frank Manaka, who had traded houses with Flora Woods. Interviewed April 18, 1996.

ED RICKETTS, JR., remembered many stories of his father, his lab and connection with Steinbeck. Interviewed August 5, 1995, August 25, 2005.

JIMMY RODRIQUEZ was the policeman on the Cannery Row evening beat from 1937 to 1942. Interviewed October 21, 1995, April 20, 1996, December 26, 1996.

DOROTHY (DOTTIE) BICKNELL SANCHEZ is Gabe Bickwell's oldest daughter. Interviewed December 9, 2004, February 15, 2005, January 21, 2005, March 26, 2006.

THOMAS STEINBECK is the son of John Steinbeck. Interviewed August 19, 2005.

U.S. ARMY. Correspondence September 21, 2005.

FLORUS WILLIAMS was Red Williams' younger brother. Interviewed August 26, 1987.

JIM WILLOUGHBY was a lifelong resident of Pacific Grove, whose father was the custodian at Hopkins Marine Station. Interviewed August 26, 1997.

ELENA YOUNG grew up in Cannery Row in the late 1930s and 1940s. Interviewed October 25, 1995.

NOTES

1. John Steinbeck, *The Log from the Sea of Cortez*, Viking Press (1951), "About Ed Ricketts."

2. Interview by Michael Hemp on February 21, 1983 with Grace Bergara.

3. From a telephone interview with Ed Ricketts, Jr., by Pat Hathaway on May 25, 2005.

4. John Steinbeck, *The Log from the Sea of Cortez*, Viking Press (1951), "About Ed Ricketts."

5. Monterey County Courthouse, County Clerk's Office, property transfer records, June 22, 1937, between Yee King and the Pacific Biological Laboratories, Inc.

6. Jackson J. Benson, *The True Adventures of John Steinbeck, Writer*, Penguin Books (1984).

7. *Monterey Cypress*, November 21, 1896.

8. *Monterey Trader*, November 22, 1935.

9. *Monterey City Directory*, 1911.

10. From an interview with Sparky Enea by George Robinson on February 14, 1973. Sparky, a fisherman, accompanied Steinbeck and Ricketts on their voyage to the Sea of Cortez in 1940.

11. *Monterey Peninsula Herald*, August 19, 1993, article by Bonnie Gartshore.

12. Monterey County Courthouse, County Clerk's office, marriage license of Flora Woods and Santiago Domenech, September 9, 1818.

13. Monterey County Courthouse, County Clerk's office, divorce decree of Flora Domenech and Santiago Domenech, October 1, 1923.

14. Monterey County Courthouse, County Clerk's office, property transfer records show that on March 7, 1928, Flora Domenech bought the property at 799 Ocean View Avenue from the Monterey Investment Company.

15. From an interview with "Mary" by George Robinson in 1975. "Mary" had been one of Flora's girls in the 1930s and had seen the two men in Flora's.

16. Tom Mangelsdorf, *A History of Steinbeck's Cannery Row*, Western Tanager Press (1986).

17. *Game and Gossip* magazine, May 9, 1953.

19. *Monterey Trader*, December 13, 1935.

19. From an interview with "Mary," one of Flora's girls, by George Robinson in 1975.

20. From an interview with Sparky Enea by George Robinson on February 14, 1973.

21. Monterey County Courthouse, County Clerk's office, property transfer records, May 26, 1936.

22. Katharine A. Rodger, *Renaissance Man of Cannery Row*, University of Alabama Press (2002).

23. Tom Mangelsdorf, *A History of Steinbeck's Cannery Row*, Western Tanager Press (1986).

24. Monterey County Courthouse, County Clerk's office, death certificate of Flora Adams, August 1, 1948.

25. John Steinbeck, *The Log from the Sea of Cortez*, Viking Press, (1951), "About Ed Ricketts."

26. From an interview with Sparky Enea by George Robinson on February 14, 1973.

27. U.S. Census, 1920: Monterey, California.

28. Ibid.

29. Monterey County Courthouse, County Clerk's Office, property transfer records, June 18, 1918, between King Fook Wing and the Wing Chong Co.

30. Sandy Lydon, *Chinese Gold: The Chinese in the Monterey Bay Region*, Capitola Book Co., (1985).

31. *Game and Gossip* magazine, May 9, 1953.

32. John Steinbeck, *Cannery Row*, Viking Press (1994).

33. Interview by Michael Hemp on May 14, 1987, with Charlie Nonella.

34. Susan Shillinglaw, Ph.D., Introduction to *Cannery Row*, Penguin Books, 1994.

35. San Mateo County Clerk's Office, marriage license.

36. Monterey County Courthouse, County Clerk's office, birth certificate for Harold David Bicknell.

37. Monterey County Courthouse, County Clerk's office, Bicknell divorce records.

38. A copy of this letter was provided by California Views: The Pat Hathaway Photo Collection.

39. Interview by Michael Hemp on May 14, 1985, with Charlie Nonella.

40. Interview by the author on March 25, 1996, with Dick Shaw, grandson of Flora Woods, who had been a cannery worker.

41. John Steinbeck, *The Log From the Sea of Cortez*, Viking Press (1951), "About Ed Ricketts."

42. Interview by Michael Hemp on May 14, 1985, with Charlie Nonella.

43. Michael Hemp, *Cannery Row: The History of John Steinbeck's Old Ocean View Avenue*, The History Company (1986).

44. Monterey County Courthouse, County Clerk's office, property records.

45. Correspondence from Gabe Bicknell to a Mr. Dahl in 1949.

46. Monterey County Courthouse, County Clerk's office, death certificates.

47. From an interview of "Mary" by George Robinson in 1975.

48. Ibid.

49. Jackson J. Benson, *The True Adventures of John Steinbeck, Writer*, Penguin Books (1984).

50. John Steinbeck, *The Log from the Sea of Cortez*, Viking Press (1951), "About Ed Ricketts."

51. Interview by Michael Hemp on February 21, 1983, with Frankie Bergara.

52. Interview by Michael Hemp on April 27, 1987, with Jimmy Rodriquez.

53. Interview by Michael Hemp on March 20, 1984, with Charlie Nonella, who took Hemp to the spots on the Carmel River where he and other collectors gathered frogs for Ed Ricketts.

54. Correspondence to the author on March 21, 2006, from Dennis Copeland, archivist for the California Room, Monterey Public Library.

55. Michael Hemp. *Cannery Row, the History of John Steinbeck's Old Ocean View Avenue*, The History Company (2002).

56. Interview by Michael Hemp, on May 14, 1985, with Charlie Nonella, who for years was a cannery worker and had a great knowledge of the people and events of Cannery Row.

57. Correspondence to the author on October 21, 2004, from Pat Hathaway.

58. Katharine A. Rodger, *Renaissance Man of Cannery Row*, University of Alabama Press (2002).

59. Bruce Ariss, *Inside Cannery Row*, Lexikos Press (1988). Bruce Ariss first met John Steinbeck in 1934. They became friends and Ariss and his wife, Jean, accompanied Ed Ricketts and Steinbeck on their trip to Mexico in 1936.

60. Ibid.

61. Katharine A. Rodger, *Renaissance Man of Cannery Row*, University of Alabama Press (2002).

62. John Steinbeck, *The Log From the Sea of Cortez*, Viking Press (1951), "About Ed Ricketts."

63. Ibid.

64. Ibid.

65. Correspondence to the author on March 20, 2005, from Bettina Hotelling, who related taking a walking tour of Point Lobos with Jean Ariss, the wife of Bruce Ariss, who showed her the tide pool where she and Ed found the dead girl.

66. Nelson Valjean, *John Steinbeck: The Errant Knight*, Chronicle Books (1975).

67. *Monterey Peninsula Herald*, March 3, 1933.

68. During a meeting of the Ocean View Avenue Gang on May 2, 1997, in Ed's lab, Frank Wright, who had known Ed Ricketts, reported that when he asked Ed if the frog party occurred, Ed told him it did not.

69. Anna Ricketts, *Recollections*, an unpublished book written in 1984. Provided courtesy of Ed Ricketts, Jr.

70. Jackson J. Benson, *The True Adventures of John Steinbeck, Writer*, Penguin Books (1984).

71. John Steinbeck, *The Log From the Sea of Cortez*, Viking Press (1951), "About Ed Ricketts."

72. Interview by Michael Hemp on October 3, 1986, with Charlie Nonella.

WHILE VISITING CANNERY ROW, I STOOD OUTSIDE OF KALISA'S WITH A GLASS
of red wine, whose contents I hoped would help me see better into the rapidly approaching

dusk and light fog. I heard the sound of a door closing, perhaps across the street. I turned toward Ed Ricketts' lab, and there was Doc coming down the stairs. From the look on his face, he was a man with a purpose. His path was toward Lee Chong's grocery and I bet myself another glass of wine that he was going for several quarts of his favorite beer, Burgermeister.

He entered Lee Chong's, and I walked the short distance to its front door and looked in. Doc had taken two quarts of Burgie out of the icebox, nodded to Lee behind the adjacent counter and was coming toward me at the door—I won my bet.

1998. The author sits where Gabe Bicknell did in 1945.
MICHAEL K. HEMP

I stepped back from the door to let Doc pass. And as he did so, I could swear that he gave me a brief but knowing look. That look made me feel good. By now, the fog had thickened a bit, but I could see Doc walking to the lab. I later realized I had unconsciously waved goodbye.

Doc was walking up his steps, when I heard a commotion that seemed to come from up the street past the vacant lot. Through an opening in the fog, I saw a car pull up in front of a dark wooden building. Three or four men piled out of the car and I clearly heard one tell the others, "This is Dora's place. Let's go in."

I had just about finished the glass of wine I'd won when the darkness and fog began to reclaim Cannery Row for another night. I turned toward La Ida, but before I walked off, the men who had gotten out of the car went up the porch stairs to enter the building. The fog thinned and I thought for a moment that the wooden building had been replaced with one of gray concrete. The fog swirled in and the dark wooden

2005. The parties in Ricketts' lab. This gathering was for John Steinbeck's birthday. Left to right, Michael Hemp, the author, Art Ring and Thor Rasmussen.

building reappeared. To my left, I saw some lights come on in the lab and I knew Doc would be working late that night.

A feeling of calm came over me and I knew I was now a true believer.

· · ·

My extensive research showed that the people, places and events in *Cannery Row* were mainly real; however, my favorite description of the book and the Cannery Row area is far more mystical than factual. This particular description came from *California—Searching for the Golden State*, by James D. Huston.

> That is what the book and what the film set out to explore, a place somewhere on the coastlines of our imaginations. If it exists at all, you will find it most days, floating offshore in the fog, out there just beyond the reach of the camera, or in the softened light as early sun begins to break up the fog—floating above the water in that kind of light. A glorious mirage, an ecosystem of the mind.

—A.L. "SCRAP" LUNDY
Santa Barbara, California
2008

ACKNOWLEDGMENTS

ON BEHALF OF MYSELF AND ALL THOSE WHO ENJOY THIS BOOK, I WISH TO express my deepest appreciation to the people and institutions that so kindly provided the information and photographs that made this book possible. I valued every contribution, large or small, as of equal importance. Therefore, I have listed all contributors alphabetically in order to avoid unintentionally giving more credit to some than others.

THERESA ACCOMAZZO—For helping develop the structure of the book, as well as editing for Angel City Press.

RACHEL BARAJAS—Photo scanning

DON BARTHELMESS—Photo transfers

ROBBY BARTHELMESS—Encouragement to continue writing

FRANKIE BERGARA—Frankie worked in the canneries in the 1930s and 1940s, knew Ed, and was able to contribute valuable insights before he died.

JOE AND DORIS BRAGDON—Joe was a late-1930s cannery worker who knew Ed Ricketts, and Doris was a resident of Pacific Grove in the 1930s. Both contributed valuable information.

JAMES BRIDGES—Graphic designer, a member of the Cannery Row Foundation Board of Directors and an accomplished artist who was of critical help in the early stages of this project.

KATHIE STACKPOLE BUNNELL—The daughter of well-known photographer Peter Stackpole, who graciously gave permission to use some of her father's photos of Cannery Row.

PADDY CALISTRO AND SCOTT MCAULEY, ANGEL CITY PRESS PUBLISHERS—I am most grateful to Paddy, Scott and their excellent staff for making this book possible. Without their unabashed enthusiasm and desire to make the book "the best it can be," I seriously doubt if the book would have been published. Thank you, Paddy and Scott.

STEVE COOK, PH.D.—A dedicated professor of English Literature at Westmont College in Santa Barbara, California, who has a deep appreciation of Steinbeck's writings. Steve had a seemingly endless amount of patience in editing and helping me see the need to make a stronger connection between this book and *Cannery Row.* Steve's insightful knowledge and appreciation of *Cannery Row* made this connection come to life, especially in the feelings he conveyed in the summaries of each chapter.

DENNIS COPELAND, CALIFORNIA ROOM ARCHIVIST AT THE MONTEREY PUBLIC LIBRARY—Provided many photos and difficult-to-obtain information.

BRUCE DUNCAN—Encouragement to start the book.

THE FAMILY HISTORY CENTER AT THE SANTA BARBARA CHURCH OF LATTER DAY SAINTS—A wonderful group of volunteers who aided me in obtaining U.S. Census data.

BOB FAULKNER—Graphic designer, whose interest in the project and skillful design abilities were very significant factors in the early stages of this book.

TOM FORDHAM—Without realizing it, Tom introduced me to the book *Cannery Row* and to John Steinbeck. I am forever grateful to him.

BONNIE GARTSHORE—A gifted reporter and local historian who really believed in the true history of Cannery Row. I miss her friendship and knowledge.

ETHEL GEARY OF AFFORDABLE OFFICE SUPPORT—Word Processing.

KAREN HARTFIELD—For her constant encouragement and much-needed editorial assistance.

PAT HATHAWAY—One of California's leading historical photo archivists, very knowledgeable about Cannery Row and always willing to help with photos and information.

MICHAEL K. HEMP—The founder of the Cannery Row Foundation, a Steinbeck and *Cannery Row* authority, good friend, and the person who enabled me to become a *Cannery Row* true believer.

HISTORICAL SOCIETY OF HENRY COUNTY, INDIANA—provided information on Harold "Gabe" Bicknell's early life in New Castle, Indiana.

NEAL AND BETTINA HOTELLING—Steinbeck authorities and providers of valuable information.

BILL HYLER—As a former cannery worker and part-time assistant for Ed Ricketts, Bill provided valuable information on Cannery Row.

BILL JOHNK—Master craftsman who built exact replica scale models of many of Cannery Row's principal buildings. Bill provided difficult-to-obtain information on the Wing Chong Co. building.

KATHY KIKKERT—For artfully designing this book and bringing my vision to reality.

KURT LOESCH—Unknowingly started me on my path to becoming a *Cannery Row* true believer.

IRENE LONGUEIRA—Lived in Cannery Row from 1920 to 2002, and was able to provide critical eyewitness information that would not have been otherwise available. Irene passed away in 2002, leaving a huge empty spot on the Row.

ROBIN MATTHEWS—In addition to her word-processing capabilities, she had the ability to establish order out of the confusion and chaos I constantly created. Without her ability in this regard, the book could not have been completed.

THE MESA CAFÉ PATIO TABLE THREE LITERARY ROD AND GUN CLUB (AND SHAWNA, THE VERY CAPABLE WAITRESS)—All of you constantly provided pithy comments.

MONTEREY COUNTY CLERK'S OFFICE—Over my ten years of research, the very friendly and competent staff made finding records enjoyable.

KALISA MOORE—"The Queen of Cannery Row" and operator of the former Kalisa's (La Ida), a former president of the Cannery Row Foundation and always willing to help.

MELISSA MOORE—For her help developing the structure of this book.

EDWARD RICKETTS, JR.—As the son of Ed Ricketts (Doc), Ed, Jr., was an eyewitness to life in his father's lab; as a result he was able to provide valuable information that otherwise would not have been attainable.

JIMMY RODRIQUEZ—The policeman on the evening Cannery Row beat from 1937 to 1942. Jimmy provided eyewitness information that was not otherwise available. Because of his generosity of spirit, his knowledge of Cannery Row will continue to be shared despite his passing.

DOROTHY "DOTTIE" BICKNELL SANCHEZ—Gabe Bicknell's oldest daughter. Dottie lived in Cannery Row during the 1930s and 1940s, knew Flora Woods and Ed Ricketts, and had first-hand knowledge of the antics her father that Steinbeck used to create the bums Mack and Gay.

DICK SHAW—A cannery worker in the late 1930s and the grandson of Flora Woods, Dick provided valuable information about his grandmother before he died.

SUSAN SHILLINGLAW, PH.D.—Scholar in Residence at the National Steinbeck Center in Salinas, California, a professor of English at San Jose State University and a Steinbeck scholar of international renown. I am very grateful that she cared enough for this book to read the manuscript and offer very valuable suggestions.

GAIL STEINBECK—The all-important link to Angel City Press. Gail has always been my ardent supporter. Without her, there would be no book.

FLORUS WILLIAMS—Red Williams' younger brother provided interesting eyewitness information on John Steinbeck and Gabe Bicknell. It was fortunate that before he passed Florus shared so much of the history that only he knew.

JIM WILLOUGHBY—Son of the custodian at Hopkins Marine Station. Before he died Jim provided a more accurate version of his father, inspiration for the watchman in *Cannery Row*.

FRANCIS YEE—Widow of Jack Yee, the son of Won Yee. Mrs. Yee provided valuable information on the family grocery store, Wing Chong Co.

ELENA YOUNG—Daughter of Irene Longueira, Elena grew up on Cannery Row. She and her friends knew Ed Ricketts and Gabe Bicknell. As a result she was a knowledgeable observer of life on Cannery Row.

—A.L. "SCRAP" LUNDY
Santa Barbara, California
2008

APPENDIX

CANNERY ROW:
THE SUMMARY
BY STEVE COOK, Ph.D.
Professor of English, Westmont College

SUMMARIES OF TEXTS ARE, FOR THE MOST PART, SUMMARIES OF WHAT HAPPENS: a sequence of events in a narrated work driven by a plot. They assume the story as a whole is reflected in a series of occurrences comprising the arc of a story and its outcome. However, looked at through such a peephole, *Cannery Row* would appear to be plotless at times. There does not appear to be any overarching story so much as there are a number of stories that quite often do not appear to satisfactorily follow from one another. Nothing noticeable seems to have been set in motion by any event, issues, or problem that must be overcome by any of the characters. No life-changing events occur and none of the characters change. They just seem to have been lifted onto the threshold of the reader's consciousness and left there to either crawl onto the pages by themselves—or not.

Depending on which peephole you choose, the stories comprising *Cannery Row* often seem incongruous. However, just as it might seem misleading to summarize *The Grapes of Wrath* as a story about the Joad family's Depression-era struggle to journey westward from a parched Oklahoma dust bowl to the "Promised Land" of California, so might it be misleading to summarize *Cannery Row* as an incongruously episodic, regional story about the quirky inhabitants of a cannery-lined waterfront place known as Cannery Row in Monterey, California, in the mid-1930s.

Summaries of *Cannery Row*'s chapters seen from a single peephole assume they provide an adequate perspective of what drives the storyline. However, everything in the real Cannery Row, "warped and woven into a fantastic pattern" is "warped and woven into [the] fantastic pattern" for which *Cannery Row* has become a symbol. Like the place Cannery Row itself, the Word Cannery Row yields a "fabulous place." The pattern provided by both real place and Word, "extends [our] wonder of both." It is a many peepholed wonder, literally and figuratively revealed when "the tide goes out" and the "quiet, lovely world" of Cannery Row can be found "set down alive."

THE SUMMARIES

JOHN STEINBECK'S OPENING CHAPTER in *Cannery Row* is not numbered, but simply headed by the noun "Cannery Row." Instead of beginning with a linear narrative like that of the Joad family in *The Grapes of Wrath*, the opening pages of *Cannery Row* read more like a prelude that begins by invoking Cannery Row as simultaneously an actual place in Monterey, California, as well as ". . . a poem, a stink, a grating noise, a quality of light, a tone . . . a dream." Elements like sardine canneries, honky-tonks, whorehouses, little crowded groceries, restaurants and flophouses are intoned as if they were diverse sacraments in a communion. Given no more or less status than any of the other elements making up this "fantastic" communion are those ordinarily presumed higher in the food chain of social acceptability: a marine biologist (named Doc), girls (from Dora Flood's brothel), cannery workers (scurrying to harvest the day's catch), a Chinese grocer (named Lee Chong), a foraging Modernist artist (named Henri), and a gaggle of bums (named Mack and the boys), lounging in the shade of a large Monterey cypress tree.

Curiously enough, as present in the narrator's mind as the actual people and places of Cannery Row are, the narrator whimsically hypothesizes about how he might be able to "set down alive" the real people, places, and events embodying Cannery Row. In thinking out loud how to do so, the narrator invokes the fragility of certain sea-worms to infer there are, like certain delicate marine organisms, some words which can ". . . break and tatter under the touch," making it almost impossible to capture what they represent. Regardless, his hope is that the narrative would move closer to rendering life whole—but how? "By opening the pages [of his narrative]" he says, "and letting the characters crawl in by themselves."

CHAPTER ONE: Lee Chong and his grocery, which is "a miracle of supply," are the major focus of Chapter One. "A worried gentleman named Horace Abbeville" shoots himself on the fish meal in the warehouse he used to settle the sizeable food bill owed Lee Chong. Later in the chapter, Lee Chong's "new" warehouse becomes the prize in a game of wits between Lee and Mack. At stake is whose perception of the newly acquired warehouse will prevail: Lee's of the warehouse as an investment, or Mack's of it as a home for himself and the boys. As Lee and Mack verbally play out their hands, Lee feigns being out-maneuvered, and resigns his grocery and warehouse to the benign and mutually supportive protection offered by Mack and the boys. They then claim the warehouse by renaming it the "Palace Flophouse and Grill."

CHAPTER TWO: Technically, Chapter Two is called an "interchapter," a term coined to account for chapters in *The Grapes of Wrath* which struck many readers as objectionably incongruous with what was going on with the "main" storyline about the sharecropping Joad family. The problem surfaces again with the seemingly "random" lines opening Chapter Two of *Cannery Row*: "The Word is a symbol and a delight . . . which sucks up men and scenes, trees, plants, factories, and Pekinese. Then the Thing becomes the Word and back to Thing again."

The purpose for such interchapters in *Cannery Row* is the same as in *The Grapes of Wrath*: to universalize something at once particular and central to the main characters, but not exclusive to them.

After the casual lines about Doc getting a beer from Lee Chong's which end Chapter One of *Cannery Row*, Chapter Two's incongruous opening sentences foster the impression of an interchapter. The "plot" of Chapter Two is to re-introduce the narrator's concern ending the opening chapter entitled "Cannery Row": how to write the stories embodying *Cannery Row* so that they are not just lifelike, but "alive."

CHAPTER THREE: Dora Flood and her "stately whorehouse" are specifically located on the Row, and both are characterized as large, fair and great. Dora's beneficence in the face of overly pietistic town authorities is reflected in her ". . . unsung, unpublicized, shameless dirty wages of sin [that] lead the list of donations" to ". . . charities, hungry children . . . jobless fathers and . . . worried women." One of Dora's former watchmen, William, is rebuffed in his attempts to become part of the community comprised of Mack and the boys who conclude ". . . [William] was too far beneath them." He dies after sticking an ice pick in his own heart in front of Lou, Dora's Greek cook.

CHAPTER FOUR: An old Chinaman with brown, deep-set eyes appears on the Row each dusk, descending the same path down to the pier pilings where he disappears each evening, only to emerge again each dawn. The sound of his flip-flops melodically flapping along marks his descent down to the pilings each night at dusk and his subsequent ascent at dawn. Andy, a ten-year-old "beautiful boy," tries to challenge the Chinaman by marching behind him and mocking his inscrutability by shrilly chanting "Ching-Chong Chinaman sitting on a rail— 'Long came a white man an' chopped off his tail." However, Andy is reduced to whimpering as his challenge is met by something unfathomable; he sees—or imagines he sees—the old Chinaman become "one huge brown eye big as a church door." Through the exotic peephole of this single eye, Andy imagines he can see a landscape bereft of life, embodying a "desolate, cold aloneness."

CHAPTER FIVE: This chapter adds more to our sense of Doc and his lab, Western Biological Laboratory. Just as Lee Chong's grocery was a "miracle of supply," so is Doc's lab, only instead of groceries it supplies biological specimens, care-giving, and a ". . . fountain of philosophy and science and art in the Row." His lab is also where he lives, simultaneously as inhabitant, owner, operator, and sometime-dispenser of wisdom. Thus the narrator somberly notes that Doc has a face that is ". . . half Christ and half Satyr." Having ". . . dug himself into Cannery Row" like a hermit crab or a gopher, Doc is perceived as someone whose "sympathy had no warp;" everyone who knew him wanted . . . to do something nice for Doc."

CHAPTER SIX: Chapter Six immerses the reader in the intertidal connectivity created by the symbiotic relationships between a dizzying array of marine life in ". . . a Great Tide Pool on the tip of the Peninsula." The tide pool becomes the focal point for a Socratic dialogue between Doc and Hazel. Intellectually slow by conventional standards, Hazel has a different perspective that remains free of conventional assumptions and results in "interesting" questions. As Doc and Hazel work the tide pool for specimens, Hazel asks Doc, "[why] . . . stink bugs got their asses up in the air?" Doc replies with implied incredulity, "I think they're praying." However, in the next breath he puts what would appear to be his own presumptuousness in perspective when he adds, "the really incredible thing is that we find it remarkable."

CHAPTER SEVEN: Chapter Seven chronicles the development of the Palace Flophouse. Beds find their way into the areas Mack partitioned out for each tenant with chalk. Art from Henri's chicken feather period, gilded cattails, Coca-Cola calendars with coke-bottle-figured blondes and a ". . . silver scrolled monster [stove] with floriated warming ovens and a front like a nickel-plated tulip garden" all endear the Palace Flophouse to its inhabitants. Eddie, an understudy bartender at La Ida, contributes a "winin' jug." The ever-changing contents of the jug inspire the boys' sentiments toward Doc to materialize in the form of a plan to throw him a party, the expense of which will be borne by getting ". . . a nickel apiece for frogs" that Mack and the boys intend to hunt down.

CHAPTER EIGHT: Chapter Eight is a droll tale about the Malloys who, like a pair of hermit crabs, move into an abandoned shell of a boiler outside the Hediondo Cannery. The boiler has all the accoutrements of home except curtains, which Mrs. Malloy longs for. Not to be denied, Mrs. Malloy buys curtains for $1.98, a "set with curtain rods thrown in," despite Mr. Malloy's belaboring the obvious: their boiler's ". . . got no windows."

CHAPTER NINE: After Doc and Hazel return from the tide pool with sacks of starfish, Mack successfully maneuvers Doc into unknowingly revealing a way to fund the secret plan to ". . . do something nice for [him]": selling frogs, three or four hundred priced at a nickel apiece. Mack trades on Doc's patronage of Lee Chong's in an effort to get the transportation needed to go on the "hunt" for the frogs. Though perhaps even more wary of Mack's seeming "altruism" than Doc, Lee Chong bargains with Mack, letting him have the use of his old truck that no longer works if Gay, one of the boys, will fix the old Model T.

CHAPTER TEN: Frankie is an awkward, perhaps even developmentally challenged eleven-year-old boy who is desperate for a place, not in a physical sense but a place in someone's heart or affections. Inevitably, the place Frankie came to covet most was with Doc. Doc tries to help Frankie by feeding him with opportunities to become part of the larger community of the Row, but Frankie's various neuropathies catch up with him. The chapter ends with Frankie spilling a tray of beers in front of Doc's party guests, and then fleeing into Doc's basement. Horrified, Frankie burrows like a frightened rodent into the bottom of an excelsior box, whimpering as he struggles to leave his sense of shame and imagined loss behind.

CHAPTER ELEVEN: Having overcome some of the logistical hurdles to an all-out assault on the frog community in rural Carmel, Mack and the boys, particularly Gay and Eddie, tame the quirks and jerks of Lee Chong's Model T truck. After the truck breaks down, Gay disappears for six months on a quest to find a needle valve to fix the truck. The only news the boys get of Gay in the interim is of the police finding him asleep in Holman's Department Store display window, with different colored shoes on.

CHAPTER TWELVE: Famous humorist Josh Billings dies in the Hotel del Monte in Monterey. Shortly thereafter a dog is seen dragging several yards of human intestines with a stomach attached out from the gulch next to the French-educated Doctor's adobe. In the Adobe Bar several outraged citizens, sensitive to even the hint of a slight against a citizen of their town, decide to confront the French-educated Doctor of ". . . sickness, birth and death . . . [practicing on] animals . . . and embalming."

CHAPTER THIRTEEN: Eddie finds a working needle valve for Lee Chong's Model T. A red rooster is "accidentally" run over and purposely put to use in a stew of windfall carrots and onions. A roadside feast, complete with transforming food smells, evening light, and the "winin' jug" becomes a prelude to more detailed plans for Doc's party. The idyllic morning of planning is interrupted by a landowner who, after some initial hostility at the cooking fire on his land, is befriended by Mack, who doctors the landowner's tick-bit bitch and makes permanent friends of both (the landowner and his dog; the ticks died.)

CHAPTER FOURTEEN: The "hour of the pearl" is described and elaborated upon in this chapter. The phrase refers to a quality of light on the waterfront produced by the changing luminescence between the first hint of light and an early dawn. The results are described as a soft light which runs from gray to silver, and its effect, like its namesake the pearl, can transform the ". . . tin and iron and rust and splintered wood, chipped pavement and . . . junk heaps, [and] sardine canneries of corrugated iron" into "a poem . . . [and] a dream." The effect is also internalized by the languor of two soldiers and their dates, who ignore a watchman who warns them to get off the little romantic spot they've found fronting the Hopkins Marine Station. The reader is left with an image of two young couples frozen in time.

CHAPTER FIFTEEN: In gratitude for doctoring his tick-bit pointer bitch, a landowner presents Mack with a puppy that will become Darling, "the mascot of the Palace Flophouse and Grill" in a subsequent chapter. The landowner also directs Mack and the boys in their quest for bountiful nickel-apiece frogs, to what could only be described as a tune-up for the frog Armageddon. The hunt is christened beforehand by some Prohibition corn whiskey. What follows is a reversal of what we are told the frogs, in their millennia-long relationship with Man, had come to expect: a contest accepted by both parties, and governed by a specific set of rules: "That is the way it is done, the way it has always been done." However, Mack and the boys have their own ideas about decorum, and in their abrogation of the old rules, it was a wonderful day for Mack and the boys, though one can't say the same for the frogs.

CHAPTER SIXTEEN: After the frog hunt in the preceding chapter, the scene shifts to Cannery Row and the development of Doc's and Dora's characters. Directly revealed through selfless acts of kindness and devotion in the middle of an influenza epidemic, both Doc and Dora's generosity shine as they risk more than just exposure to the epidemic: Dora and her girls are virtual angels of mercy to the Row's heartier but hapless breed of citizens who still, like everyone else, are vulnerable to a threat beyond their ability to control. Just as Dora's efforts and those of her girls put their livelihood at risk, Doc also goes out on a limb, putting what knowledge he has to use, even though some might see his efforts as akin to practicing medicine without a license. While Monterey's more economically secure citizens no doubt engaged in safer philanthropies, Dora and Doc show a genuine depth and breadth of caring indigenous to them as human beings who, in all humility, recognize their own humanity in the vulnerability of others.

CHAPTER SEVENTEEN: Doc's loneliness and melancholy set the tone for this chapter as he undertakes an adventurous five-hundred-mile trip to La Jolla for specimens to sell. While Mack and the boys are up in the Carmel Valley mapping out a strategy for their frog hunt, Doc begins his outing to La Jolla, but not before a flagpole skater hired by Holman's Department Store piques the curiosity of one of Salinas's inhabitants as to how he manages to relieve himself. Back in Cannery Row, before Doc has gone down the road too far, his love of hamburgers diverts him into an eatery where Blaisdell the Poet recalled what he perceives as Doc's idle talk about drinking a "beer milk shake." Taking both a surly hitchhiker and his own curiosity about beer milk shakes down the road with him, Doc is moved to action by the temperance-minded hitchhiker's unflattering response to his driving; he kicks the hitchhiker out and quickly finds a beer milk shake, ordering it from a "blonde beauty" at a nearby counter stand.

CHAPTER EIGHTEEN: After stops in Ventura, Carpinteria, and a Chicken-in-the-Rough place in Los Angeles, Doc motors on to La Jolla, where he collects more than twenty-two little octopi, several hundred sea cradles, and sees a drowned, "pretty, pale girl with dark hair," caught in the La Jolla tidal pattern. The face and the beauty of the young girl affect Doc profoundly; it haunts him like the imagined sound of ". . . a high thin piercingly sweet flute, "embodied by the young girl's still and open-eyed tranquility. His reverie is interrupted by a man who can only see the young woman in terms of what she represents as a bounty.

CHAPTER NINETEEN: First mentioned in Chapter Seventeen, a flagpole skater hired by Holman's Department Store attracts curious Salinas onlookers. None are more interested than Richard Frost who is haunted enough to go sleepless for several nights and even fight with his wife because of his preoccupation with—at first—something unnamed about the flagpole skater. Able to stand it no longer, Richard gets up late and goes out, much to his wife's consternation, for she wonders if his nocturnal wanderlust is in the direction of Flora's brothel. Richard returns, however, and tells his wife, "He's got a can there." Richard had simply wanted to know how the flagpole skater relieved himself. So, Richard got up and went down to Holman's to ask him directly—and the flagpole skater told him.

CHAPTER TWENTY: Mack and the boys finally return from the great frog hunt. Creating a provisionally different monetary system with Lee Chong based on bartering nickel-apiece frogs for booze and bread, Mack also manages to weasel party supplies out of Lee for Doc's "surprise" party. Still down in La Jolla, Doc is unaware that Mack, the boys, and other inhabitants of the Row have inadvertently started the party without him. Of course, plans often go astray and "Doc's party" gets out of hand: uninvited guests cause problems and a very territorial Mack and the boys "over protect" Doc's lair with such ferocity that Doc's lab is smashed. After the maelstrom of flying fists and furniture, Darling, the four-legged queen of the Palace Flophouse and Grill mirrors her masters' debauchery. Not content with shoe chewing and pillow shredding, Darling indulges herself like Mack, only instead of drinking and fighting, she gorges herself on a massive washtub cake baked for Doc, crawls into the crater of the cake her gorging creates, throws up, lays down in it, and falls asleep. In the meantime, the frogs taken prisoner on Mack and the boys' raid, escape their bonds and flee into the desert-sized (to them) streets of Cannery Row, and become an overnight pestilence even a Pharaoh could understand.

CHAPTER TWENTY-ONE: Doc returns with specimens from La Jolla and finds his lab in ruins. Confronting Mack, Doc punches him several times, vents his anger at him, offers him a beer—and gets over the carnage. In the process however, Doc has to listen to Mack's self-recriminations and portrait of his wife, who left Mack after "she only got hurt from [him]."

CHAPTER TWENTY-TWO: Doc and a date are interrupted by Henri the painter, who is the epitome of the Modernist movement; he is always poised to "make it new"—as long as he never has to finish "it." After a particularly terrifying version of murderous ghosts, Henri, figuratively speaking, wants Doc to look under his bed for ghosts. However, Henri's boat in which he lives has no bed anyone can look under. Despite the fact his boat has no "facilities," Henri accepts the help of Doc's empathetic date to go over to his boat and look under his non-existent bed for anything nightmarish. Doc's well-intentioned "date" ends up staying with Henri five months until the lack of facilities drives her off.

CHAPTER TWENTY-THREE: In contrast to the whimsical and laconic life aboard the painter Henri's purposely unfinished boat, Chapter Twenty-three's focus is the "black gloom" and despair hanging over the Palace Flophouse and Mack and the boys because of their complicity in the disastrous party for Doc. While other inhabitants of the Row think about taking vengeance on the Palace Flophouse's inhabitants, Doc appreciates the way Mack and the boys, "balanced on the scales of good and evil," have beaten the system. Echoing one of the early claims the omniscient narrator makes about Mack and the boys evading the "getting and spending" trap, Doc points out "They just know the nature of things too well to be caught in that . . . sale of souls to gain the whole world." Doc's largesse of spirit is complemented later in the chapter when his medical knowledge helps save the life of Darling, the Palace Flophouse mascot. That event, in some mysterious way, marks the emergence from a depression the Row as a whole was experiencing, and the resurrection of a more familiar spirit, akin to Doc's altruism. In any case, an evil that had seemed to stalk other inhabitants of the Row, one of whom lost both legs to a locomotive, was now on the run. The chapter ends with Dora's suggestion to Mack, who is still in search of atonement for the party Doc never got to, "Why don't you give him a party he does get to?"

CHAPTER TWENTY-FOUR: A whimsical portrait of a couple's tension over the supremacy of reality or the imagination. The wife, Mary Talbot, appears to be in denial of the obvious diminishment of their material lives. Her response to hardships is to be an eternal optimist and to punctuate that optimism by keeping her and her husband's spirits up—by throwing tea parties for her cats. The husband, Tom Talbot, though buoyed by Mary's insistence that she and her husband are "magical people" and can work their way out of any tight situation, finally loses patience and says, "I'm sick of pretending everything . . . I'd like to have it real." Real, for him, means an empirically experienced baked ham instead of the pictures of one his wife has cut out and put on their plates after she served them on a platter. The response of Mary Talbot to her husband's looking through a single peephole, his "either-or" approach, is, of course, another party with the family cats "Kitty Cassini" and "Kitty Randolph." This time, however, the "horror" of what her husband deems is "real" and the consequences of Mrs. Talbot's romantic imagination is brought home midparty by Ms. Kitty Cassini; she reverts to jungle form, and stabs an uninvited mouse with a claw, but at least does so "daintily." Mr. Talbot has to finish the mouse so it won't continue being tortured by Kitty Cassini but, proving chivalry—and romance—are not dead, asks his wife to turn her back while he dispatches the mouse.

CHAPTER TWENTY-FIVE: A change comes over Cannery Row: the "black gloom" created earlier by Mack's widely felt guilt about the consequences of Doc's party, assorted illnesses in the Row, and a drop-off in business at Dora's, seems to have dissipated like the coastal fog. Previously convinced ". . . misfortune had crept into every crevice," of the Row, everyone just as suddenly becomes "lousy" with the kind of good feeling that breeds success. Mack is encouraged enough to start rolling his version of Sisyphus's rock—a new party that has been repackaged as a birthday party Doc will get to—up Cannery Row. Everyone and everything felt the joy diffusing the Row: sea lions, the Palace, Hermann's hamburger stand, the San Carlos Hotel, even Gay in the county lockup over in Salinas. However, the only obstacle to giving Doc a birthday party he will get to is that no one knows his birthday. Mack rises to this challenge and plays his trump card: circumlocution. While a wary Doc knows Mack's verbal poker means he's up to something, Doc doesn't know what. With a sagacity born out of experience, Doc gives Mack a false birth date, allowing Mack to think he has succeeded.

CHAPTER TWENTY-SIX: Joey and a companion named Willard play like two Lilliputians peeping out on a giant's world. Though not trapped like the "babies in bottles" both have heard are in Doc's lab, both nevertheless seem bottled up within themselves: Willard by an emotionally predatory "relationship" with Joey, and Joey by having to play host to Willard's parasitic needs. For example, although Joey sees a penny on the ground first, Willard shoves him aside and snatches up the penny. After Joey objects, Willard caustically mocks him, telling him to ". . . go take some rat poison," referring to Joey's father, who chose rat poison to end his life.

CHAPTER TWENTY-SEVEN: Having forgotten he had given Mack a false date for his birthday, Doc seems oblivious to preparations going on all around him for a party in his honor. However, he becomes aware that something is going on concerning him; he just doesn't know what. Doc's party, referred to as "the party" by its planners—which means just about everyone in the Row—takes on mythical status in anticipation of its actually happening. Even Gay, still over in the Salinas jail, hears about it. Unfortunately—a drunk asking a bartender about "the party" is overheard by Doc, and suddenly "everything [falls] into place." Displaying his sagacity once more, Doc makes preparations by putting away what he doesn't want broken in the lab, and lays in enough food for a regiment. To help Doc, since nickel-apiece frogs had become scarce after their diaspora in the streets of Cannery Row, fifteen tomcats had been lured into captivity by a female cat "in an interesting condition."

CHAPTER TWENTY-EIGHT: The young boy named Frankie reappears. Still wanting to convey how much he worships Doc by getting him something for the party, Frankie foregrounds his admiration of Doc by making him a present of a black onyx clock with a statue of St. George killing the dragon atop it. So desperate is Frankie to show his affection for Doc that he doesn't even think about the consequences of smashing the window of Jacob's Jewelry Store to get the clock. Of course Frankie is caught but, since he obviously cannot control himself, the police tell Doc that Frankie will probably have to be institutionalized, not just cited for vandalism or theft. Thinking Frankie had a reason for his behavior, Doc asks him, "Why did you take it?" After looking at Doc for a long time, Frankie tells him, "I love you." This time it is Doc who flees, but not down into the cellar below his living room; he ends up instead "in the caves below Pt. Lobos," collecting.

CHAPTER TWENTY-NINE: Everyone, now including Doc, is waiting for what everyone but Doc thinks is a surprise for him, a birthday party on what ostensibly is his birthday: October 27. However, it is neither a surprise, nor will it be his birthday. Against the backdrop of ". . . the gray time between daylight and street light, "everyone waits for the party to begin happening: Dora at the Bear Flag with her freshly dyed orange hair, Doc indulging his "sweet and sickly mood" by constructing his own Eleusinian Chant out of *Pavane to a Dead Princess, Daphnis and Chloe,* and the *Moonlight Sonata,* and Mack and the boys at the Palace with a problem in logistics: how, unseen, to get twenty-one tomcats to Doc's.

CHAPTER THIRTY: What do a twenty-five-foot-long string of firecrackers and a bunch of China lily bulbs, a well polished connecting rod and piston out of a 1916 Chalmers, a pincushion-turned-artwork titled "Pre-Cambrian Memory," a rowing machine and six beer glass doilies, twenty-one tomcats, and a patchwork silk quilt all have in common? All are presents to be offered up to Doc at his party. The "surprise" celebration begins and then quickly grows into something robust, but just as quickly dwindles, despite being fueled by Benny Goodman tunes, Eddie's tap dance, and Doc serving the provisions he had laid in. The party winds down even further into an inward sadness and contemplation as Doc chants eight passages of poetry translated from the Sanskrit and "everyone remember[ed] a lost love, everyone a call." The poetry, however, only serves as a coda to fan the flames of the Eleusinian spirit of the party until it enjoyed ". . . all the best qualities of a riot."

CHAPTER THIRTY-ONE: A lonely gopher in his prime—similar to Doc in several ways— embarks on a new stage of life. The gopher prepares his burrow (home) and gathers mallow stems (riches) for the love of his life in an upscale neighborhood (for a gopher)—but ". . . no female appeared." Frustrated, the gopher makes provocative sounds to attract a female, maintains his territory by fighting a scarred and embattled old bull gopher, and resignedly moves into "a dahlia garden where they put out traps every night."

CHAPTER THIRTY-TWO: The morning after his "surprise" birthday party finds Doc cleaning up the party wreckage in his lab to the Gregorian music of a *Pater Noster* and an *Agnus Dei*. As incredibly pure and sweet, ". . . angelic, disembodied voices filled the laboratory," Doc picks up the volume of poetry from which he read out loud the night before, and reads six more lines to "the sink and the white rats, and to himself." The notion created by what Doc chooses to read, the Gregorian music, and images like "waves splash[ing] on rocks they had not reached in a long time," suggests that our "last" view of Doc—and by extension Cannery Row—may be more of a coda. Whatever the experience has been with Cannery Row in *Cannery Row,* it is not over. Instead, like the speaker in the poem itself, all know that there has been ". . . full in our eyes the hot taste of life" that is Cannery Row. Our last view of Doc and Cannery Row, however, is of rattlesnakes which "lay still and stared into space with their dusty frowning eyes" behind glass in Doc's lab. As Doc reads and the narrative ends, there is thrown over the whole of the scene as well as the last chapter, a tonality or mood as diaphanous and as full of promise as the "hour of the pearl."

RECOMMENDED READING LIST

Ariss, Bruce. *Inside Cannery Row: Sketches From the Steinbeck Era in Words and Pictures.* San Francisco: Lexikos, 1988.

Hemp, Michael Kenneth. *Cannery Row: The History of Old Ocean View Avenue.* Monterey: The History Company, 1986.

Lynch, Audry. *Steinbeck Remembered.* Santa Barbara: Fithian Press, 2000.

Mangelsdorf, Tom. *A History of Steinbeck's Cannery Row.* Santa Cruz: Western Tanager Press, 1986.

Rodger, Katharine A. *Renaissance Man of Cannery Row: The Life and Letters of Edward F. Ricketts.* Tuscaloosa: University of Alabama Press, 2002.

Shillinglaw, Susan, Ph.D. *A Journey into Steinbeck's California.* Berkeley: Roaring Forties Press, 2006.

Shillinglaw, Susan, Ph.D. *Introduction to Cannery Row.* New York: Penguin Books, 1994.

Steinbeck, John. *The Log From the Sea of Cortez,* (the narrative portion of the book *Sea of Cortez* by John Steinbeck and E. F. Ricketts, 1941), reissued with a profile, "About Ed Ricketts." New York: Viking Press, 1951.

Tamm, Eric Enno. *Beyond The Outer Shores: The Untold Odyssey of Ed Ricketts, the Pioneering Ecologist Who Inspired John Steinbeck and Joseph Campbell.* New York: Four Walls Eight Windows, 2004.

INDEX

ANGEL CITY PRESS